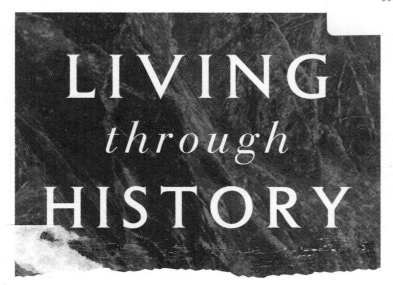

# LIVING *through* HISTORY

# The Twentieth Century World

Nigel Kelly, Rosemary Rees
and Jane Shuter

Heinemann

## Acknowledgements

Published in Great Britain by Heinemann Library,
Halley Court, Jordan Hill, Oxford, OX2 8EJ
a division of Reed Educational and Professional
Publishing Ltd.

OXFORD CHICAGO PORTSMOUTH (NH) USA
BLANTYRE MELBOURNE AUCKLAND IBADAN
GABORONE JOHANNESBURG

Heinemann is a registered trademark of
Reed Educational and Professional Publishing Ltd.

© Nigel Kelly, Rosemary Rees and Jane Shuter
1998

The right of Nigel Kelly, Rosemary Rees and Jane
Shuter to be identified as the authors of this
work has been asserted by them in accordance
with Copyright, Designs and Patent Act.

First published 1998

02 01 00 99
10 9 8 7 6 5 4 3 2 1

## British Library Cataloguing in Publication data

Kelly, Nigel, 1954-
   Twentieth century world.- (Living through
   history)
   1.History, Modern - 20th century - Juvenile
   literature
   I.Title II.Rees, Rosemary, 1942- III. Shuter, Jane
   909.8'2

ISBN 0 431 06857 7 (Hardback)
ISBN 0 431 06856 9 (Paperback)

Designed and produced by Visual Image.
Illustrations by Sally Artz, Stephen Wisdom and
Visual Image.

Printed in Spain by Edelvives

## Photographic acknowledgements

The authors and publisher would like to
thank the following for permission to
reproduce photographs:

AKG: 2.1A, C, 2.4D
Punch/Centre for the Study of Cartoons: 2.4A
Bridgeman: 1.2B
Corbis: 2.11D
e.t. Archive: 1.3E, 2.13H
Getty: 2.5A, F
Hulton Getty: 1.4B, 2.1B, 2.3D
Imperial War Museum: 1.2C, E, 1.3C, 1.4H, 2.3B,
2.8A, C, p143, 2.11A, 2.12B, 2.14F
Katherine Jenerette: 3.6C
Katz: 3.4D
Kobal Collection: 3.3B
Liddle Collection/University of Leeds: 1.3B
David Low/Centre for the Study of Cartoons:
3.5C, 3.6A
Magnum: 2.9A
Mary Evans: 1.3A, 1.4A, C, 2.10B
Mirror Syndication: 2.10C
Museum of London: 1.4G
Nationalmuseet Denmark: 2.7B
Popperfoto: 2.10A, 2.11E, 2.14A, 3.3A
SCR: 2.7D
Topham: 2.14E
Yad Vashem: 2.14B

Cover photograph: Bridgeman/Manchester City
Art Library, Imperial War Museum

The publishers have made every effort to trace
copyright holders of material in this book. Any
omissions will be rectified in subsequent
printings if notice is given to the publisher.

The authors and publisher would like to thank
Mrs E W Vaughan Williams for sharing her
memories of the Second World War with us and
for generously allowing us to use family
memorabilia.

# CONTENTS

## *Twentieth Century World*

### The changing world

The twentieth century has been a time of upheaval and very rapid change. As the maps on these two pages show, the world in the 1990s is very different from the world as it was at the beginning of the century. The major powers no longer own huge empires in Africa and Asia and almost all of the old colonies have gained independence.

### *World powers in 1900*

In 1900 the richest and most important powers were Great Britain, Russia, France, the USA, Germany, Austria Hungary, Italy and Japan.

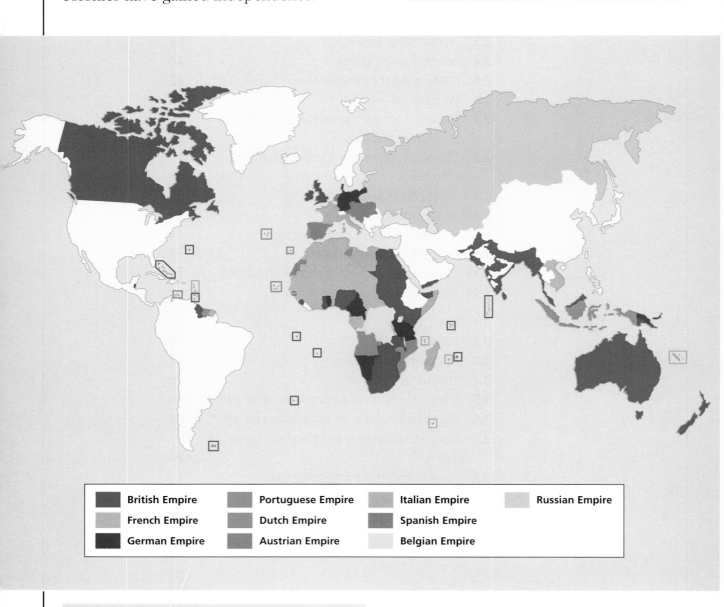

| | | | |
|---|---|---|---|
| British Empire | Portuguese Empire | Italian Empire | Russian Empire |
| French Empire | Dutch Empire | Spanish Empire | |
| German Empire | Austrian Empire | Belgian Empire | |

The world in 1900.

## From colonies to trade

At the end of the twentieth century, the power of a nation is measured not by how many colonies it has, but by how much influence it has on world affairs. This influence comes mainly as a result of a country's wealth. The United States, for example, is the most influential country in the world, and is also the wealthiest.

### World powers in the 1990s

In the 1990s the countries with the largest share of world trade were the USA, Germany, Japan, France, Italy and the UK. The richest countries were Switzerland, Japan, Finland, Luxembourg, the USA and the United Arab Emirates.

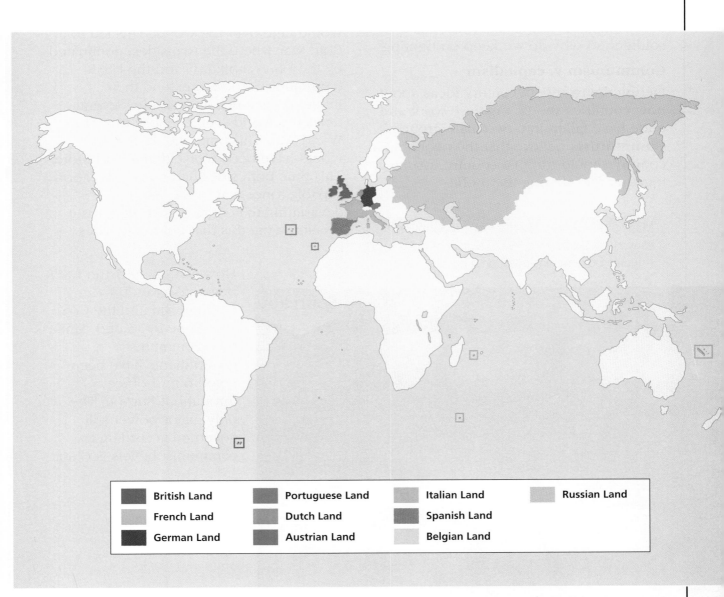

| | | | | | | | |
|---|---|---|---|---|---|---|---|
| British Land | | Portuguese Land | | Italian Land | | Russian Land | |
| French Land | | Dutch Land | | Spanish Land | | | |
| German Land | | Austrian Land | | Belgian Land | | | |

The world in 1997.

## Always at war?

The twentieth century has seen two major world wars (1914–18 and 1939–45). It is also true that in almost every year of the century there has been war in some part of the world. Even as you read this there are many places in the world where fighting is taking place. One question you need to consider as you read this book is why are there so many wars? We know that warfare today kills innocent civilians as well as soldiers, so why do we keep on fighting?

### Communism v. capitalism

During the twentieth century ideas about how countries should organise work and trade have fallen into two main groups: **Communists** believe that the people in a country should run that country, working together and sharing the profits.

Capitalists believe that there should be workers and bosses. The bosses provided the capital (money to set up factories and workshops) and so get all the profits.

This argument spilled over into how countries should be ruled, too. After the Second World War ended, in 1945, the governments of countries took one side or the other. They did not trust each other. They felt that, sooner or later, one belief would take over the world. This led to a Cold War where the two sides, dominated by the USA (capitalist) and the USSR (communist), tried to extend their influence as much as possible. Several times the world seemed close to a Third World War. This time, the destruction would have been worse than ever before. This time both sides had nuclear weapons capable, once war broke out, of devastating the entire planet. Perhaps it was knowing this that held both sides back.

However, in 1991 the USSR began to abandon communism and the Cold War came to an end. Since then communist governments have been voted out of office throughout Europe. The only major power still governed according to communist beliefs is China.

Many modern wars are civil wars, fought with conventional weapons. Here soldiers of the Angolan government question a possible rebel.

**Source A**

## A shrinking world

Conflict and mistrust have been big issues in the twentieth century. But there have been more positive issues too. Medical discoveries meant that diseases that were killers in 1900 are now easily treated. People have also worked together in technological research. In the 1900s there were still areas of the world unexplored. Now people can survey the whole world from satellites in space, and are exploring space itself. They can communicate with places on the other side of the world, almost instantly, using satellites.

## The developing world

Many of the poorest countries in the world are countries that broke away from European empires, and could not develop their economies quickly enough to support themselves. The contrast between their poverty and the wealth of 'developed' countries has led to them being called 'the Third World', because life there is so different. Many people in these developing countries hover on the edge of starvation much of the time. They have much shorter life expectancies and little to cushion them if they are hit by natural disasters, like floods or droughts. Despite help from some developing countries many people in developing countries do not have clean drinking water, access to medical care, or anything like enough to eat.

### Source B

### 1900–1998

**World population**

| 1900 | 1998 |
| --- | --- |
| 160,000,000 | 5,925,770,871 |

**Average life expectancy**

| 1900 | | 1998 | |
| --- | --- | --- | --- |
| Men | 45 | Men | 73 |
| Women | 48 | Women | 79 |

**Life expectancy, 1998**

| | |
| --- | --- |
| Republic of San Marino (highest) (developed country) | 85 |
| Rwanda (lowest) (in Third World) | 36 |

### Things to think about

Think about the things we use in everyday life that were not widely used in 1900. For example, what would your life be like without:

electric light and power, central heating, computers, TVs, videos, music centres, batteries, planes, cars, motorways, cinemas, fast food, washing machines, dishwashers, microwaves?

In the 1990s it is easier than ever to talk to people and collect information from all over the world, especially using computer technology.

# 1.1 THE FIRST WORLD WAR 1914–18

## Why was there a war in 1914?

The war that broke out in 1914 had been brewing for a long time. The most powerful countries in Europe were rivals for power. Who had the biggest empire? Who was selling the most iron? Who was building the most ships? Could they stay in front? Would they have to fight to stop someone else taking part of their empire? As soon as one country started to build up its army and navy, the others felt they had to do the same. They formed alliances with each other, promising to help each other if war broke out. They made plans about what to do if they were invaded. In 1914 there were two sides:

**The Triple Alliance**: Austria-Hungary, Germany and Italy.

**The Triple Entente**: Britain, France and Russia.

**Source A**

## The spark for war?

Europe was tense, ready for war. Once war broke out, the alliances would make sure that all the major powers became involved. On 28 June 1914 Franz Ferdinand, son of the Austrian emperor, was shot in Sarajevo, Serbia. Serbia was in the Balkans, a part of Europe that Russia and Austria-Hungary had struggled over for years. Serbia was friendly with Russia, not Austria-Hungary. A Serb shot Franz Ferdinand. So Austria-Hungary invaded Serbia. Russia was ready to help Serbia. Germany was ready to help Austria-Hungary. France had agreed to help Russia. Britain held back, hoping not to get involved. Italy too was uncertain what to do. Finally, in 1916, it joined the war against Germany and Austria-Hungary (it hoped to gain land from Austria-Hungary at the end of the war).

## The first move

Kaiser Wilhelm II, the German ruler, felt his army and navy were better prepared than those of his enemies. He declared war on Russia on 1 August and on France two days later. He had to defeat France quickly before Russian troops attacked his eastern border. So he decided to invade France. To do this he had to cross Belgium. In 1839 Germany and the other major powers had signed a treaty promising not to invade Belgium. The Kaiser asked the Belgians to let his army march through to attack France. Belgium refused. The Kaiser felt that he had no choice. He invaded Belgium on 3 August 1914. Britain declared war on Germany the next day, saying that Belgium needed protecting. Really the British were fighting to stop Germany becoming too powerful. Countries in the Empire, such as Canada and New Zealand, also joined the war on Britain's side.

A pre-war Italian cartoon, showing the Kaiser as greedy for an empire.

## Where did they fight?

### The Western Front

Germany's war to the west. Here Germany fought Britain, France, their colonies and (after 1917) the USA.

The trenches were on the Western Front.

### Battle of Jutland

The only big battle at sea. Neither side a clear winner.

### The Eastern Front

Germany's war to the East. Here Germany fought the Russians. There was no fixed line of battle here, the front line shifted back and forth over many miles. The Russians fought while they were also having a revolution which replaced their king with a communist government.

### Submarines

The Germans used submarines to sink ships bringing supplies to Britain and her allies. When they sunk the *Lusitania*, a US passenger ship that was also carrying war supplies, the USA decided to join the war against Germany.

### The Middle East

The war in the Middle East revolved around which side controlled the Suez Canal, which joined the Mediterranean to the Red Sea.

### Italy

In 1914 Italy had been on Germany's side. In 1915 the Italians changed sides. So Germany had to fight Italy, too.

### The Colonies

There was also fighting in the German colonies in Africa. The 3 colonies marked here were captured by the allies.

## Who had what in 1914

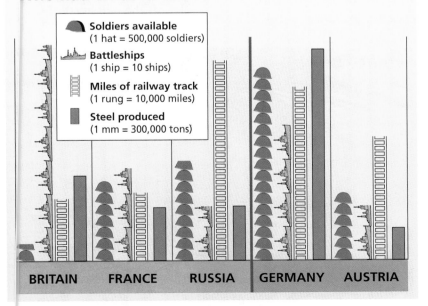

**Soldiers available**
(1 hat = 500,000 soldiers)

**Battleships**
(1 ship = 10 ships)

**Miles of railway track**
(1 rung = 10,000 miles)

**Steel produced**
(1 mm = 300,000 tons)

BRITAIN   FRANCE   RUSSIA   GERMANY   AUSTRIA

## Gavrilo Princip

Gavrilo Princip assassinated Archduke Franz Ferdinand and his wife. He was a student and a member of the Serbian resistance group called The Black Hand.

Asked why he shot Franz Ferdinand, he replied:

*Because people suffer so much. It is the Archduke's fault. ... I am not sorry for what I have done.*

## Over by Christmas?

Both sides expected the war to be 'over by Christmas'. It lasted 54 months and swallowed up over 10,000,000 lives. At least 20,000,000 more people were wounded or crippled. Why did the war drag on so long? For many reasons, one of them being the form of warfare used.

## Digging in

One element of First World War warfare was the trenches that both sides dug to protect themselves. At first, trenches were just ditches deep enough to protect the soldiers. But it became clear to both sides that, on the Western Front, their soldiers would be stuck in the trenches for some time. Once they were in the trenches, they were able to keep each other pinned down with machine-gun fire. So they put boards down for the soldiers to walk on and lined the trenches with sand bags, to make them stronger. They made dug-out holes at the back of the trenches, for men to rest in. Some German trenches even had concrete dug-outs and electric light!

The trenches spread right across Europe from Switzerland to the North Sea, in a muddle of zig-zagging lines. Most fighting was done from front-line trenches. Behind them were support trenches, then reserve trenches. All these trenches were connected by narrower communication trenches.

## No Man's Land

Enemy front-line trenches could be as little as 20 metres apart or as much as over a kilometre apart. The land between enemy trenches was called No Man's Land. As soon as winter arrived, it became a churning mass of shell craters, mud and corpses. Told to **consolidate** his position, one officer replied: *it is impossible to consolidate mud.*

### Source A

Corporal C. R. Russell remembers fighting on the Western Front.

When you were at the front line there would be two companies in the support trench and one in the front line. After three or four days you would change around.

All along the winding trench you'd have three men in a bay. One was on guard, one was cleaning up the trench, trying to improve it, and one was having a sleep. You changed round each hour, so you got to sleep an hour out of three, unless the guard saw something, when you all jumped up and started firing. That was at night. It was the same in the day, except you got the periscope out now and again, so you could see. We didn't bother much, because Jerry [the Germans] didn't come across much in daylight. So days were pretty quiet. We let off the odd burst of fire and they'd reply, but that was it.

### Source B

A painting by the war artist John Nash of a trench on the Western Front at Oppey Wood. It was painted in 1918.

## Trench warfare

Soldiers fought with rifles, bayonets and hand grenades. Big artillery guns fired heavy shells at enemy trenches. Shells could do a lot of damage, but the artillery guns were not accurate and their shells could only be expected to hit in the general area of a target.

The most deadly weapons were machine guns, which fired hundreds of bullets fast and accurately. One German machine gunner said of the Allied soldiers who came out of the trenches into No Man's Land: *they went down in their hundreds. You didn't have to aim, just fire into them.*

## Source C

Canadian soldiers at the Third Battle of Ypres in 1917. They are using shell holes for cover.

### New weapons

**Gas**: Various poisonous gases were pumped into the trenches. They attacked the eyes, the insides and the nerves of the people who breathed them in. Some gases killed, others blinded and maimed. Gas was first used by the Germans in 1915; it was terrifying. But it could be a problem to the people who used it, if the wind changed and carried it back to them. The invention of gas masks helped cut its effectiveness.

**Tanks**: Tanks were huge armed vehicles with caterpillar tracks. They could cross rough ground and barbed wire with ease. Machine guns did not bother them. Tanks were first used by the Allies in 1916 and terrified the Germans. But they stuck in mud, got very hot and were death traps if a well-aimed grenade or shell hit them.

**Planes**: Planes were expensive to build. They were dangerous to fly (made of wood and canvas, with no parachutes for the pilots). But they were the most successful of the new inventions. They were first used to find out where enemy troops were. Plane design improved. Pilots became more skilful. Machine guns were put on planes so they could fight. In 1917 the Germans designed a plane that could carry heavy bombs to drop on enemy towns and cities.

## Source D

From *A Working Party*, a poem by Siegfried Sassoon, who fought in the trenches.

Three hours ago he blundered up the trench,
Sliding and poising, groping with his boots.
Sometimes he tripped and lurched against the walls
With hands that pawed the sodden bags of chalk.
He couldn't see the man who walked in front;
He only heard the drum and rattle of feet
Stepping along barred trench boards, often splashing
Wretchedly where the sludge was ankle deep.

### Pictures of war

Film was made of the war but the equipment was bulky and hard to set up. Most images - even supposed action scenes - were posed. Cameras were also big and awkward to use. War artists were sent to make official paintings and sketches of the war for newspapers.

All images of the war were censored. They were part of the propaganda war. People who showed unchecked images of the war faced prison if caught. They could not show the full horror of events until the war was over.

## The Liverpool Scottish in the trenches

The Liverpool Scottish Battalion were a territorial battalion – they were formed to protect Britain from invasion, not fight abroad. But they were soon swept up into the fighting on the Western Front. Robert Scott Macfie's letters home (in *italics*) let us follow the battalion through training, the first days in the trenches and the battles of Hooge and the Somme.

### Numbers of soldiers killed, wounded or missing in three major offensives

| | | |
|---|---|---|
| **Verdun (1916)** | French: | 550,000 |
| | German: | 434,000 |
| **Somme (1916)** | French: | 200,000 |
| | German: | 500,000 |
| | British: | 420,000 |
| **Third Battle of Ypres (1917)** | British Empire | 310,000 |
| | German: | 300,000 |

## Source E

Robert Scott Macfie.

### The beginning

*Today we have been told to be ready to go abroad on Friday 30 October. We are nowhere near ready: we have damaged rifles, many men are short of clothing and equipment. Headquarters is in confusion, lots of us are recruits and the rest are imperfectly trained. I never saw so incompetent a set of officers.*

On 2 November they set off, jammed into a boat that, twelve hours after leaving England, was *going round in slow circles outside Le Havre.* They then had a long, slow, crowded journey to their training camp, in France, but a long way from the front line.

### Trenches

*We have had our first practice digging trenches. They are not at all what I imagined and must be most uncomfortable in hot weather. I expect the scientific Germans will put in hot water radiators before the cold weather comes.*

### Moving up

*We moved to a little village and joined the remains of several regiments which have been almost wiped out. The farm where we are staying is a sea of mud, ankle deep, and the roads are like rivers of yellow soup.*

### Christmas 1914

*It is Christmas Eve and we are all very homesick. The men are in an empty barn, cold and draughty, and have hardly recovered from our spell in the trenches.*

*We have been able to dry our wet clothes, and even beat off some of the baked-on clay, but we are dispirited. We are waiting to march off to even less comfortable lodgings, 'dug-outs' – holes in the ground badly roofed and full of straw.*

*We went into the trenches cold and wet, for there was heavy rain and snow as we marched there from our muddy farm. When we came out we were colder, wetter and ever so much muddier. We must have looked like Siberian exiles, not soldiers. We wear whatever we can get, not smart uniforms, and have buckets and enamel cups and mugs tied to our belts with string. We do not march, we slouch along. We hang our heads and go along at irregular intervals in twos and threes. Many of the men fall behind, because they are lame.*

The Liverpool Scottish, in action at Hooge.

### Hooge (1915)

The attack at Hooge began on 16 June 1915. Macfie was in charge of the camp:

*We got ready for the return of the troops. We set out letters, parcels, candles and food. We got tea and pea soup going on the cookers. 130 of my company had left: I was ready to feed them when they got back.*

*At last we heard the distant sound of pipes and after a while a handful of men came through the gate. Their uniforms were tattered, their faces blackened and unshaven, their clothes stained red with blood and yellow with the fumes of gas. I shouted for Y Company – only one man came forward. It was heartbreaking. Gradually others tottered in, some wounded, all in the last stages of exhaustion. By 5.30 a.m., six hours after they had all marched out, there were 25 of my men in camp. Since then I have found out that 11 were killed and 68 are in hospital. 25 are missing. I fear most are dead.*

### The Somme (1916)

A year later the Liverpool Scottish were involved in one of the most famous battles of the war – the Somme.

*Our attack, in the early hours of 9 August, was directed against a village which has been attacked several times before, and several times since, always without success. Our performance was no exception: of my company 177 went up [joined the battle] – 20 were killed, 42 wounded; about 8 are missing, probably dead. The lack of preparation, the vague orders, the ignorance of what we were supposed to do, even of the geography of the place, the absurd haste, the horrid mistakes – it was all scandalous. After two years of war it seems that our higher commanders are still without common sense. In any well-run organisation one of the divisional commanders would have been shot for incompetence – here they just send another regiment to do the same job in the same muddling way. It is worse than Hooge, much worse – and it is still going on.*

### For King and country

When the war broke out, the British army had about 164,000 men. By 1916 there were over 2,000,000. Men went off to fight, for their king, for their country, and to defend 'gallant little Belgium'. Everybody wanted to be involved in this war against the bullying Germans. Or did they?

### Against the war

Some people were against the war. Some of them didn't want to fight a war against Germany. Some were pacifists – they felt all war was wrong. They had a hard time of it. The government was trying to get all men to join up. Ordinary people would stop men who weren't in uniform as they walked down the street and ask why they were not in the services (army, navy and air force). Sometimes they even handed them white feathers, a sign of cowardice.

### Conscription

Casualties were high in the war. Despite the huge intake of volunteers, more men were needed to fight. So the government brought in conscription in 1916. They passed a law that all single men aged 18 to 41 had to join the services. Later they made married men join up, too. Men who were doing important war work in Britain did not have to join up. The government also said that men with a 'conscientious objection' to the war (beliefs that stopped them from joining up) did not have to go.

### 'Conchie' or coward?

Conscientious objectors had to go to a **tribunal**. This was supposed to listen to their arguments and decide if they were really 'conchies' or just 'cowards'. In many cases the tribunal was just a way of trying to bully people into joining up. There were about 16,000 conscientious objectors. Many refused to fight but went to war as ambulance drivers, hospital workers and stretcher carriers. About 1500 of them refused to have anything to do with the war at all. Some of these were sent to prison. Others were forced into uniform. If they still refused to fight, they were tried for treason. Some were sent to prison. Others were shot.

**Source A**

## TO THE
# YOUNG WOMEN OF LONDON

Is your "Best Boy" wearing Khaki? If not don't **YOU THINK** he should be?

If he does not think that you and your country are worth fighting for—do you think he is **WORTHY** of you?

Don't pity the girl who is alone—her young man is probably a soldier—fighting for her and her country—and for **YOU.**

If your young man neglects his duty to his King and Country, the time may come when he will **NEGLECT YOU.**

Think it over—then ask him to

# JOIN THE ARMY TO-DAY

Printed by Gerald Allen & Sons Ltd., Harrow, London, etc.

### Pressure to join up

The government put constant pressure on men to join up. Government posters told men to protect their country and their families. They told women to make their men join up. They even suggested that those who did not join up were making the war last longer, because if they joined up, the war would end and the killing would stop.

A poster pressurising women to get their boyfriends to join up.

## ONE 'CONCHIE'S' WAR

Howard Marten was living in London at the start of the war. He was a Quaker, and Quakers did not believe in fighting. He registered as a conscientious objector. He was forced to join the Non-Combatant Corps (who did not fight, but worked at jobs like driving ambulances, instead). He and a group of others were put in prison in Harwich for refusing to obey orders. They were then shipped out to France. This made their position very dangerous. Disobedience 'in the field' was punishable by death.

Marten and four others were court-martialled for disobedience. Marten was surprised at the sympathy of those running the trial. Perhaps they were too sympathetic – the verdict was never announced and there was a re-trial. They were led out to the parade ground to hear their fate:

*There were lots of men lined up, mostly Non-Combatants and labour battalions. We were taken to one side of it, then led out, one by one, into the middle of the square. I was the first of them and until my verdict was read, no one knew what was going to happen. An officer in charge read out the various crimes: refusing to obey a lawful command, disobedience at Boulogne and so on, then: 'The sentence of the court is to suffer death by being shot.' There was a pause. I thought, 'Well, that's that.' Then he said 'Confirmed by the Commander-in-Chief'. 'That's double sealed it now,' I thought. Then, after a long pause: 'But commuted to penal servitude [prison] for ten years.' And that was that. What was good was that we were back in England and out of the hands of the army.*

Marten was sent to prison, then he was released to do useful war work in a stone quarry at Dyce, near Aberdeen.

Howard Marten, photographed with his mother and Cornie Barret, one of the other 'conchies' sentenced to death with him.

### *Arthur Evans*

Arthur Evans was one of the conchies sent to France in May 1916, along with Howard Martin.

*Howard Martin and I were put in a foundry making parts for railway lines. We all refused to obey any orders given us by officers. So we were put in prison to be tried for disobedience. A day or two before the trial a captain came to see me and said, 'I've just left the company office with your papers - they're marked 'death' in red at the top. Do you intend to go on with this?' I said 'Yes, you see, sir, men are dying in agony in the trenches for things they believe in. I wouldn't do less than them.' To my utter astonishment he saluted me, then shook me by the hand and left.*

### Deserters and mutineers

If there was one thing worse than a conchie, as far as the army was concerned, it was a deserter (a soldier who ran away) or a mutineer (a soldier who rebelled against his officers). Yet the realities of the war, the inept way it was conducted and the horrific loss of life meant that many people who began by supporting the war turned against it.

### Covering up

The government was furious when people who had been in battle turned against the war. They didn't want people at home finding out how bad things were. Everyone had to pretend, put on a brave face. Soldiers who went home on leave often felt very isolated. They had seen the realities of war, but in Britain most people were still talking about a different war, one that ignored the harsh realities of bad commands, appalling conditions and senseless waste of life.

This painting, *The Harvest of Battle*, was painted by the war artist C. W. R. Nevison. He made sketches at the time, but the painting was not finished until 1921. He would probably not have been allowed to show it in war-time.

### SIEGFRIED SASSOON

Siegfried Sassoon was the generals' worst nightmare. He joined up as soon as the war started. He became an officer and led his men bravely into battle. He was given the Military Cross medal.

But Sassoon was appalled at the way the generals threw away lives for what he thought was no good reason. He wrote poetry about the horrors of war. In 1917 he threw away his medal. He refused to fight any more. He wrote to *The Times* newspaper, saying:
*I am making this statement as an act of defiance of military authority as I believe the war is being deliberately prolonged by those who have the power to end it.*

The army didn't want to court-martial a soldier who had won a medal. They tried to get Sassoon to tone down his criticisms. They excused him by saying that he had shell-shock from battle. They put him in a military hospital in Scotland, until he 'recovered'. While the army hoped he would 'come to his senses', Sassoon tried to get support for his anti-war views. But he felt more and more guilty about being 'out of it' while men were fighting and dying, so he returned to the front and survived the war.

Source C

An Australian recruiting poster. Troops from all over the colonies fought in the war. Some of them, like the Canadians, accepted the British army could court-martial their men. Others, like the Australians, did not.

## Who was shot?

Three hundred and forty-six men were shot for military offences between 1914 and 1916. Most of them were ordinary soldiers. Three were officers. Many of them had been at the front for many months, had fought and suffered in the trenches, and one day just snapped.

## Why were they shot?

The army shot deserters and mutineers as a lesson to everyone else. They had to make it more dangerous to run away from battle, or refuse to go into battle, than it was to take part. The lists of those shot were read out to all soldiers 'on parade'.

## Source E

Captain Slack was an officer in the East Yorkshire Regiment. He had to organise at least one firing squad.

There was one poor little man who came to me. He was posted to my Company, ran away, was caught and ran away again, deserted, and he was court-martialled to be shot. My Sergeant-Major and I had to pick ten men to shoot him, which we did, and one of my officers had to be in charge with a revolver.

The man was shot. I wrote to his mother 'killed in action'; I think that's what they were all told. I wasn't at the execution. I didn't want to be. It wasn't a nice job for the ten men, either. My Sergeant-Major organised it. I didn't go into the details, if he was put on a chair and blindfolded, or the mark over his heart, I didn't go into the details at all. It was a horrible thing to have to do, but it had to be done.

### Pardoned?

In November 1997 the government pardoned at least some of the 307 soldiers executed for desertion or cowardice during the First World War. It is now accepted that many had shell-shock. Two examples:

**Joseph Byers**, aged 17, had lied about his age to join up when he was 16. He was shot for being absent from parade. Those who were in the shooting party were crying as they fired; it took three attempts to kill him.

**James Archibald**, aged 20, said to be 'of poor intellect', ran away. Many of those executed were said to be of 'low intelligence'.

## Who were the suffragettes?

Suffragettes was the name given to women who demanded the right vote in elections. (Suffrage means being allowed to vote.) There were many different groups, who did not always agree about the best way to get support. The National Union of Women's Suffrage Societies (NUWSS), set up in 1897, wrote letters to MPs and held dinners to try to get support. They believed in convincing people gradually. Individual politicians gave them some support, but Parliament was very divided on the issue of votes for women and no one considered it very important. In 1903 the Pankhurst family set up the Women's Social and Political Union (WSPU). Their motto was 'Deeds Not Words'. They were nicknamed 'suffragettes', a name which soon applied to all women demanding the vote.

## What did they do?

The WSPU wanted publicity. They had a uniform of purple, green and white. They went on marches, held public meetings, printed their own newspapers. They went to factories and mills to speak to ordinary women. They got noticed. More and more women joined; old and young, rich and poor. But Parliament did not give them the vote. So the suffragettes did things to get arrested. They felt, rightly, that people would be shocked at them being treated as criminals. They got more support, but not the vote. Some became more **militant**. They smashed shop windows, set fire to pillar boxes, even homes (as long as they were empty). This lost the movement a lot of support. Many of their members felt they had gone too far and resigned. By the time the First World War started, suffragettes had become very unpopular.

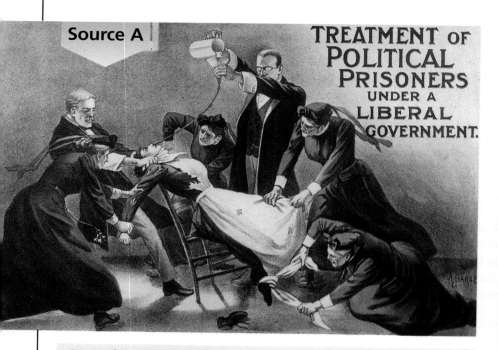

**Source A**

TREATMENT OF POLITICAL PRISONERS UNDER A LIBERAL GOVERNMENT.

Some of the suffragettes went on hunger strike in prison. The government said they should be forcibly fed, through a tube up the nose. This action horrified many people and gave suffragettes more support.

### Forced feeding

The government said forced feeding was a 'necessary medical treatment'. *The British Medical Journal*, 1912, disagreed:

*Prisoners were held down by force, tied to chairs or bedsteads while the tube was forced up their nostrils. After each feeding the pain of insertion is worse, because of the damage already done by the tube.*

*One prisoner was found to have pneumonia and pleurisy as a result of this treatment in prison. This cannot come under the category of 'necessary medical treatment'.*

**Source B**

## THE PANKHURSTS

Emmeline Pankhurst and her daughters, Christabel, Sylvia and Adela set up the WSPU. They took the lead in most of the activities of the movement, including being arrested. Christabel was one of the first to urge militant action.

The Pankhursts did not always agree over tactics. Sylvia and Adela wanted to push harder for working women to be given the vote. Emmeline and Christabel argued that it was more important to get the vote for some women first. This was best done, they argued, by getting the vote for the 'respectable' women who made up most of their membership. Working women who wanted the vote could not campaign in work hours. They also had the most pressure from their bosses and their families not to become suffragettes. This disagreement led to Sylvia being thrown out of the WSPU in 1914. Adela had already been talked into leaving when she became ill and kept losing her voice through all the public speaking.

## FREDERICK PETHICK-LAWRENCE

Not all men were against women getting the vote. Frederick Pethick-Lawrence, a lawyer, advised the suffragettes on their legal rights, helped edit the newspaper *Votes for Women* and helped set up their printing business. He and his wife were arrested several times. He went on hunger strike and was force-fed.

## EMILY DAVISON

Emily Davison is one of the most famous suffragettes. She gave up her teaching job to campaign full-time for votes for women. Emily was a militant. She smashed windows and set fire to pillar boxes. She was arrested several times, went on hunger strike and was force-fed. In 1913 she went to the Derby, a famous horse race held each year. She ran onto the racetrack to try to stop the king's horse, Anmer. She was trampled and died in hospital four days later. The suffragettes said she had died for the cause and gave her a huge funeral. Sylvia Pankhurst described her as *one of the most daring and reckless of the militants*.

## What did people think of suffragettes?

Different people felt very differently about suffragettes. You cannot say 'men thought this' or 'women thought that'. People also changed their minds about suffragettes as suffragette tactics changed. Many people did not feel strongly either way.

Suffragettes and people who were against them fought hard to convince people to join their side of the argument. Militant people on each side could get very heated. Anti-suffragette posters suggested that suffragettes were frustrated women who could not get a husband, using the slogan *You don't need the vote, you need a bloke!* Militant suffragettes burned churches as well as houses. They also damaged famous paintings to make their point.

### Source C

An extract from *The Unexpurgated Case Against Woman Suffrage*, by Sir A. E. Wright, printed in 1913.

**Failure to recognise that man is the master, and why, is at the root of the suffrage movement. Suffragettes ignore man's superior strength, so they ignore the fact that government runs on compulsion. They ignore man's superior mind, so come to think that they can think as well. They ignore man's superior money-earning capacity, so ignore the power of the purse.**

### Source E

From *The Times* newspaper, covering an election in 1909.

**The suffragettes seem to have made a favourable impression on the voters here, especially the miners. Some miners would even vote for the candidate who was in favour of women's suffrage without thinking about his opinions on other subjects. This is the first election in which I have seen the voters really concerned about the right to vote – worried about the concerns of 20 or so women who are good speakers.**

A poster from the time, made for the National League for Opposing Woman Suffrage (NLOWS). Women, as well as men, joined this league – just as men, as well as women, supported the suffrage movement.

### Source D

A SUFFRAGETTE'S HOME

VOTES FOR WOMEN

AFTER A HARD DAY'S WORK!
Published by the Campaign Committee, National League for Opposing Woman Suffrage, Caxton House, Westminster. JOIN!

Opinion on suffragettes in 1913.

### Postcard propaganda

The suffragettes produced newspapers, pamphlets, postcards and other goods to publicise their ideas. Their opponents were not slow to do the same.

Some opponents were content to stress the idea that campaigning was not the 'proper' place for a woman (see Source C). Others were far cruder in their tactics. They showed suffragettes as frustrated, dried up, older women.

### Needed at last!

When the First World War broke out, men joined the army in huge numbers. Women were needed to do the jobs these men had done. They were also needed to work in factories making guns, tanks, bombs and uniforms. And they were needed to nurse the wounded. Some women volunteered straight away. But more were needed. Suddenly the government needed the organisational skills of the suffragettes.

### The Right to Serve

The government gave Mrs Pankhurst £3000 to organise women to do war-work, especially in the factories making bombs and bullets. The WSPU organised marches with new banners. 'The Right to Vote' became 'The Right to Serve'. Women took on the work that needed doing. All kinds of women worked, though poor women usually got the worst jobs. Women mined coal, made bombs, learned to be builders. They drove buses, cleaned windows and farmed the land. Hertha Ayrton invented a fan to clear gas from the trenches, so saving many lives. Women showed that, given the chance, they could do hard physical work, think as well as men and earn a wage, despite what critics said. Things would never be the same again.

Once more, the government was faced with campaigns for the right to vote. They gave in for many reasons. They wanted women to give men their old jobs back after the war, without a fuss. They had seen what women were capable of doing, so it was hard to argue that they were not capable of voting.

In 1918 all women over 30 were allowed to vote. This was extended in 1928 to women over 21, giving them the same voting rights as men.

### All in favour?

Emmeline Pankhurst felt that Germany had to be beaten at all costs. She also thought that doing war-work gave women a chance to show they were as good as men. So she stopped fighting the government and helped it.

Some suffragettes thought that she was wrong to do this. Pacifists objected, including her daughter Sylvia. Militant suffragettes were horrified at Mrs Pankhurst 'helping the enemy'. On the other hand, many people who had disapproved of the suffragettes changed their minds and supported them.

A Right to Serve march, 17 July 1915.

**Source G**

## TWO SUFFRAGETTES IN WAR

In August 1914, aged 18, Mairi Chisolm rode from Scotland to London, on her motorbike, to look for war-work. She got a job carrying messages for the Women's Emergency Corps (WEC), then went to Flanders as a nurse. The team of four doctors, four nurses, two ambulances and two drivers worked hard, but they were far from the front line. Wounded men died of shock on their way to be treated. So Elsie Knocker, a qualified nurse, and Mairi set up a first aid post just behind the front line in Belgium.

*We were there for the Belgian casualties but we also had to try to rescue the pilots who were brought down in No Man's Land. That was what we got the Military Medal for, you see. We went on foot. There weren't always stretchers, we had to hope to get them out with their arms around our necks. I strained a valve in my heart lugging men around on my back. The Belgian army ambulances were three miles behind us. But we had an ambulance of our own and I'd drive them back up in that. It was like being a grouse being fired at, you had to do it in stops and spurts, being shot at. You had to get the timing right.*

*As well as dealing with the wounded, we got men in from the trenches with boils, sore feet, all sorts of things. We slept in our clothes, ready for when the wounded came in. We went into the trenches too – poked our noses in to see that everything was all right.*

Mairi Chisolm and Elsie Knocker in Belgium.

### CAROLINE RENNLES

Caroline Rennles worked in London, making bombs. The TNT in the bombs had a strange effect:

*It turned the hair that stuck out from our caps ginger and our skin yellow. They used to call us 'canaries'. Some people were nice to us, but others used to treat us like scum. You couldn't wear anything nice to work, the powder got into it. It wore off, eventually. We didn't realise it was dangerous. Train conductors used to say 'You'll be dead in two years'. So we said 'We don't mind dying for our country'. We were so young and patriotic.*

### Charlie Marsh

Charlotte Marsh began her war-work by driving a van. A photograph of her starting up the van was used in an article called 'What Women are Doing' in *The Suffragette*. She later became the driver of David Lloyd George, Minister of Munitions.

# 1.5 THE TREATY OF VERSAILLES

When a war finishes, countries have to meet to decide what is going to happen to the losers. Will they have to pay compensation to the winners? Will they have to give up land? Or could they even be taken over by the winning side? Of course, after all the killing and damage that has occurred in a war it is very difficult for decisions to be made calmly and in the best interests of everyone involved. The Treaty of Versailles which followed the First World War is a good example of this.

In January 1919 representatives from 32 countries travelled to France to decide what should be done about the defeated nations – Germany, Austria-Hungary, Turkey and Bulgaria. The representatives met in the Palace of Versailles in Paris and their discussions took six months. None of the defeated nations was allowed a say at the conference. They had to accept what was decided. Nor was Russia invited to send representatives. There had been a revolution in Russia in 1917 and the new leaders had made peace with Germany in return for giving the Germans huge areas of land. The Russians had dropped out of the war and had set up a communist government. The victorious Allies were angry about both of these things.

## How were decisions made?

Although many countries were represented at the Versailles Conference, the decisions were really made by the three most powerful leaders. 'The Big Three' were Woodrow Wilson of the United States, Georges Clemenceau of France and David Lloyd George of Great Britain.

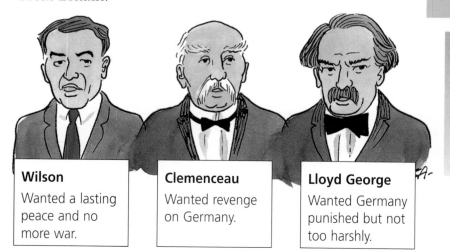

| Wilson | Clemenceau | Lloyd George |
|---|---|---|
| Wanted a lasting peace and no more war. | Wanted revenge on Germany. | Wanted Germany punished but not too harshly. |

## Lloyd-George (1863–1945)

David Lloyd-George was Prime Minister of Britain during the last few years of the First World War and represented Britain at the Versailles peace conference in Paris.

He was a Welshman who first became an MP when he was elected at Caernarvon in 1895. He stayed as that town's MP for the next 55 years!

Lloyd-George had a distinguished career in Parliament before becoming Prime Minister. He helped introduce a series of measures to improve the lives of the poor, and is particularly well known for his part in bringing in Old Age Pensions in 1908.

He was Chancellor of the Exchequer when war broke out and it was his task to make sure that Britain was in a strong enough position to fight the war.

He resigned as Prime Minister in 1922 but remained in Parliament until 1945.

## Source A

Harold Nicholson, who was one of the British representatives at the Conference of Versailles, made this comment after the treaty was signed:

**The historian, with every justification, will come to the conclusion that we were very stupid men.**

A major problem at Versailles was that the leaders had different ideas about what should happen. Wilson hoped that he could set up a fair peace and return to the United States with no risk of future war in Europe. Clemenceau, however, wanted revenge for the killing and damage that had happened in his country (where much of the war was fought). Lloyd George also wanted the Germans to be punished, but was worried that if the treaty was too harsh, the Germans would want revenge and another war would break out in the future.

Europe after the Treaty of Versailles.

Map legend:
- Territory lost by Germany to other countries
- Territory lost by Germany to the League of Nations
- Area formerly Austria-Hungary
- Area formerly owned by Russia
- Demilitarized zone

## What was decided?

The boxes below show the decisions the peacekeepers made. Neither the Germans nor any other defeated power had any say in what was decided. When the Germans saw the proposals, their Chancellor (leader) resigned in protest. But they were told that if they did not sign the treaty, the Allies would invade their country. On 28 June 1919 German representatives signed the Treaty of Versailles, but that was certainly not the end of the story!

### The Treaty of Versailles

- Germany was to agree that the war was all its fault.

- Germany was to pay **reparations** for the damage caused (later fixed at £6600 million).

- Germany was to lose its colonies, and parts of the country were given to other European nations. (One effect of this was to split Germany in two.)

- The German army was to be reduced to 100,000 men (eleven million Germans fought in the war). It was to have no air force, no tanks or submarines and only six battleships.

- Germany was not allowed to keep soldiers or build fortifications within 50km of France.

- The lands Russia gave to Germany were taken away to form new countries.

### Other decisions

- Austria-Hungary was divided into two countries.

- Yugoslavia and Czechoslovakia were set up (the peacekeepers wanted to let people of the same race govern themselves).

- Turkey lost almost all the land that it held in Europe.

The years following the First World War were dramatic to say the least. **Democratic** government came to an end in Germany; Mussolini established himself as **dictator** in Italy; and Russia saw the murder of its royal family and the setting up of a communist government.

## The Romanovs

Until 1917 Russia was ruled by a royal family called the Romanovs. The head of that family was Tsar Nicholas II. He ruled Russia with the help of nobles appointed by him as advisers, but the 95% of Russians who were peasants or town workers had no say in how Russia was run.

The Tsar and his nobles lived a life of luxury. Everyone else did not. Much of Russia's farmland did not produce enough food and industrial workers in the towns worked very long hours for very poor pay. Despite this, many Russians loved their Tsar, whom they saw as chosen by God to rule. But in the latter half of the nineteenth century opposition to the Tsar began to grow in Russia and various revolutionary groups were formed. The Tsar responded by having his secret police keep a careful eye on opposition.

## Revolution

In 1905 there was an attempted revolution against Nicholas. He was so concerned that he agreed to make changes. He even agreed to set up an elected parliament, called the Duma. But once Nicholas was confident that he was back in control, he took little notice of the Duma and carried out harsh measures against his opponents.

In 1914 Russia went to war against Germany. At first people welcomed the war, but as the army began to suffer defeats, discontent grew. The Tsar went to the front to lead the army. But this left his wife (a German) and her 'holy man' Rasputin to run the country. The Tsar became even more unpopular and a group of nobles murdered Rasputin.

## A new government

By March 1917 there were riots in the streets and the Tsar was forced to **abdicate**. A new Provisional Government took over, but in October 1917 it was overthrown by members of the revolutionary party, the Bolsheviks.

## RASPUTIN

Rasputin was a Russian peasant who saw himself as a 'holy man'. He had some interesting views, such as believing that people could only repent if they first sinned properly! Rasputin had tremendous influence over the Tsarina because he seemed to be able to help her son, Alexei, who suffered from a blood disease called haemophilia. But he was hated by the Russian nobles, who murdered him. First they poisoned him; then they put him in a sack and threw him in a river – just to make sure!

A poster issued by the Bolsheviks during the First World War. It shows the Tsar, the Church and the Russian nobility riding on the shoulders of ordinary Russians. All around are Russia's war-dead.

Source A

The Bolsheviks, led by Lenin, had great difficulty getting themselves established in power. To do so, they had to murder the Tsar and his family, and win a civil war against their opponents, who received support from most Western countries (who feared the Bolsheviks' political beliefs). Eventually Lenin changed the name of Russia to the Soviet Union and his party to the Communist Party.

After Lenin's death there was a power struggle between Stalin and Trotsky for control of the party. Stalin was eventually successful and Trotsky was exiled (and later murdered). Under Stalin, the Soviet Union was transformed into one of the world's two 'superpowers'. Yet there was a price to pay. Stalin hated any opposition. As many as 20 million people may have died for opposing his rule.

### Events in Italy

Whilst a communist dictatorship was being set up in the Soviet Union, Mussolini was establishing himself as dictator in Rome. Unlike in the Soviet Union, where Lenin and Stalin said their eventual aim was to give the workers power, Italy's dictatorship was **fascist**. Mussolini did not believe the workers should have power. He said the people should make sacrifices for the good of the nation. Amongst those sacrifices were giving up the right to trade unions and free speech.

Italy after the First World War was a country of high unemployment, strikes and demonstrations. Many people feared there would be a communist revolution. Mussolini promised strong government and was anti-communist. His support grew. In 1922 thousands of his supporters marched on Rome and demanded that Mussolini be made Prime Minister. King Victor Emmanuel agreed and appointed Mussolini.

Gradually Mussolini took more and more power. Soon he ruled, not the King. He locked up opponents and banned other political parties. He did make some improvements in Italy's agriculture and industry, but is perhaps best remembered for his foreign policy. He was determined to create an Italian empire like that of the ancient Romans. He dragged Italy into the Second World War to support Hitler and was eventually humiliated by the Allied forces. In April 1945, Mussolini was murdered and he and his mistress were strung upside down from a lamp-post in Milan.

**Source B**

Benito Mussolini, Italy's 'New Roman Emperor'.

### Lenin (1870–1924)

Lenin's real name was Vladimir Ulyanov. His parents were teachers and he was a talented student. However, when his brother, Alexander, was executed for plotting against the government, Lenin neglected his studies and became involved in revolutionary activities.

He was exiled to Siberia in 1897 and between 1900 and 1917 he spent fifteen years in exile abroad. He returned to Russia in 1917 and in November led the Bolsheviks to power. He is said to have been the creator of the Soviet Union.

## Postwar Germany

After its defeat in the First World War, Germany faced many difficulties. The harsh terms of the Treaty of Versailles caused widespread resentment in the country and the cost of reparations added to the economic problems caused by the cost of fighting the war.

Shortly before the war ended, the German Emperor, Kaiser Wilhelm, had abdicated and left the country. Germany was to have a new constitution which said that it was now to be a **republic**. Since that constitution was drawn up in the town of Weimar, historians talk of the period in Germany after the war as one when Germany was governed by the Weimar Republic.

The Weimar Republic faced many difficulties in its attempts to bring about recovery after the war:

Source C

A poster issued by the Nazis showing Hitler as the saviour of Germany.

- It had signed the hated Treaty of Versailles. It had no choice, because the Allies had said they would invade if the Germans did not sign, but that did not stop the German people from blaming the government.

- There were several attempts to overthrow the government. In 1919 there was an uprising by a group of Communists called the Spartacists. It was put down only after fierce fighting. Then in 1920 Dr Wolfgang Kapp took control of Berlin and the government was forced to flee to Stuttgart. Control was only restored because trade unions in Berlin called a general strike and no one supported Kapp.

Finally, in 1923, a young German called Adolf Hitler, and his Nazi Party, tried to carry out a putsch (takeover) in Munich. It failed and Hitler was sentenced to five years' imprisonment.

- Perhaps the Republic's greatest problems were in finding the money to make reparations payments. In 1923, after failing to persuade the Allies to reduce the payments, the government decided to stop paying them. It was trying to convince the Allies that it could not afford the payment.

The French were so angry that they sent troops into Germany's main industrial area, the Ruhr, and took coal and other products to make up for the missing payments. Encouraged by their government, the German works went on strike. The German economy collapsed and a period of **hyper-inflation** broke out. Soon people's life savings were hardly enough to buy a week's groceries!

Fortunately for Germany, Gustav Stresemann became Chancellor in 1923. He introduced a new currency, the rentenmark, and ended inflation in Germany. He also restored relations with other countries. The French left the Ruhr and in 1926 Germany joined the League of Nations. The USA lent Germany money to build up its economy and by 1928 the problems of the postwar years seemed to be a thing of the past.

## Crash

But in 1929 the American stock market collapsed and America went bust. It needed the Germans to repay the loans it had made. As a result many German businessmen went bankrupt. Similar problems occurred across the globe as the world tumbled into **recession**. Unemployment rose from below a million to over six million in Germany and the 'bad old days' of the early 1920s seemed to have returned.

Many Germans decided that the time had come for strong government. They turned to Hitler's Nazi Party. Here was a party which promised strong government. It said it would tear up the Treaty of Versailles, recover Germany's lost land and provide jobs. This was a popular message with the German people and when the Nazis won the most seats in the German Reichstag (Parliament) in 1932, Hitler was appointed Chancellor, taking office in January 1933.

### What the National Socialist (Nazi) Party believed

- The Treaty of Versailles should be torn up.
- Germany should have strong government.
- Germany should expand its territories into eastern Europe.
- The German race ('Aryans') are a master race.
- No Jews should be allowed to be Germans.

### Kaiser Wilhelm (1859–1941)

Friedrich Wilhelm Viktor Albert was Emperor of Germany and King of Prussia. He was actually related to Queen Victoria as his mother had been Victoria's eldest daughter. William received a military education and showed great determination and bravery, which helped him overcome the disability of having a withered arm. In 1888 on the unexpected death of his father he became Emperor.

In 1918, when it was clear that Germany would lose the war, there were demonstrations in Germany against his rule. He abdicated and left the country for Holland, where he lived in seclusion until his death in 1941.

## Chancellor Hitler

The German people had voted for Hitler and his Nazi Party because they wanted strong government. They were not to be disappointed. Over the next two years Hitler established a **totalitarian** state in Germany. This means that the government had control of all aspects of people's lives.

## The Enabling Act

Shortly after becoming Chancellor, Hitler persuaded the Reichstag (Parliament) to pass the Enabling Act, which gave Hitler the power to make laws and decide matters of war and peace for four years without consulting the Reichstag. In fact Hitler kept those powers permanently.

To make sure that he had full control in Germany, Hitler also banned all opposition parties and even had some of his own party murdered. The Nazis had their own private army, called the SA (Brownshirts). Hitler was concerned that the leader of the SA, Ernst Röhm, was becoming too powerful, so he had him and other leaders killed. Instead of the SA, Hitler used an élite group of the army, the SS, and the state police, the Gestapo, to root out and punish any opposition. During Hitler's time as Führer (leader), thousands of political opponents were sent to labour camps.

The harshest treatment was reserved for the Jews. Hitler used the Jews as **scapegoats**, blaming them for all of Germany's problems. He passed laws that took away their citizenship and forbade marriage (and even sexual intercourse) between Jews and Aryans (people with 'pure' German blood). Some Jews left Germany, but many did not get out in time and suffered the appalling fate of Hitler's Final Solution to the 'Jewish problem' (see pages 64–5).

## 'The young belong to me'

One of the ways that Hitler maintained his support was by using **propaganda**. The German people were subjected to a constant barrage of pro-Nazi propaganda on the radio, in the newspapers and in posters in the street. They even set up a special department led by Joseph Goebbels, called the Ministry of People's Enlightenment and Propaganda, to ensure that people 'got the message'.

But Hitler's main concern was the young of Germany. He knew that many German adults already had strong views on how Germany should be governed. The young, however, did not yet have such views, so they could be trained to think the way the Nazis wanted. This was what Hitler meant when he said that Germany's children belonged to him.

A timetable from a girls' school in Nazi Germany.

### Source D

| Periods | Monday | Tuesday | Wednesday | Thursday | Friday | Saturday |
|---|---|---|---|---|---|---|
| 8:00 – 8:45 | German | German | German | German | German | German |
| 8:50 – 9:35 | Geography | History | Singing | Geography | History | Singing |
| 9:40 – 10:25 | Race study | Race study | Race study | Ideology | Ideology | Ideology |
| 10:25 – 11:00 | Recess, with sports and special announcements | | | | | |
| 11:00 – 12:05 | Domestic science with maths | Domestic science with maths | Domestic science with maths | Domestic science with maths | Domestic science with maths | Domestic science with maths |
| 12:10 – 12:55 | Eugenics | Health Biology | Eugenics | Health Biology | Eugenics | Health Biology |

A fund raising poster for the Hitler Youth.

## Source F

Part of a newspaper article written by David Lloyd George, who was British Prime Minister at the Conference of Versailles, after meeting Hitler in Germany in 1936:

I have just returned from Germany. I have now seen the famous German leader and also something of the great change he has made. Whatever one thinks of his methods – and they are certainly not those of a parliamentary country – there can be no doubt that he has achieved a marvellous transformation in the spirit of the people, in their attitude towards each other and in their economic outlook.

One man accomplished this miracle. He is a born leader of men. He is also securing them against the constant dread of starvation, which is one of the worst memories of war and the first few years of peace.

At school, children were taught that the Führer was a great leader who should be obeyed, that Aryans were a superior race and that the Jews were to blame for all Germany's problems. Even the history books were re-written to prove this. Of course, teachers had to belong to the Nazi Teachers' Association and were dismissed if they would not join.

Education was not only for the mind. There was plenty of physical education so that boys would grow into healthy men for the army, and girls would be fit for motherhood.

Outside school, youth organisations were set up to reinforce these views. At the age of six, boys joined the Little Fellows, at ten they went on to the German Young Folk and at fourteen they joined the Hitler Youth, where they were trained as soldiers.

Girls joined the Young Maidens at six and at fourteen the League of German Maidens. They were left in little doubt that their role in life was as wives and mothers. Hitler did not approve of women going out to work, or wearing make up. But if you had lots of babies, you were awarded a special medal, the Motherhood Cross.

### Adolf Hitler (1889–1945)

After leaving school, Hitler struggled to earn a living as an artist in Vienna. He joined the German army in 1914 and won the Iron Cross during the First World War.

He was imprisoned in 1923 for leading his Nazi Party in a take-over of Munich. On his release he built up the Nazi Party until in 1933 he became Chancellor (leader of the government). His policies took Germany into the Second World War and he committed suicide just before the war was lost.

## This means war!

Hitler told the German people that he intended to tear up the Treaty of Versailles and regain the land that had been taken from Germany. He also said that he intended to win land from countries in eastern Europe (whose Slav population he considered inferior) and settle German people there. Such policies were bound to lead to war, but the other Western powers were reluctant to risk war by stopping Hitler's aggressive policies, so it was not until 1939 that war finally broke out.

## Hitler's actions

In 1933 Hitler withdrew Germany from the League of Nations – a peace-keeping organisation set up after the First World War to try to prevent such a terrible war happening again. But to succed, the League depended on its members being prepared to take action to stop a country that launched an attack on another country. In 1931 Japan had attacked China, but the League had been unable to stop Japan capturing the Chinese province of Manchuria. Two years later Mussolini attacked and captured the African state, Abyssinia. Again the League could not prevent the takeover. Hitler's withdrawal from the League showed that he did not have peaceful intentions, but the League could do nothing to stop his plans in the next few years.

Hitler soon began breaking the terms of the Treaty of Versailles. He reintroduced conscription and began building up the German airforce (the Luftwaffe).

Britain and France did little to stop him because they thought that Germany had been unfairly treated at Versailles and a strong Germany would be a good counter to the Soviet Union (Hitler hated communism).

In 1936 Hitler sent his troops into the Rhineland. This was part of Germany, but the Treaty of Versailles had said that Germany must not have troops in it. Hitler was very worried about the reaction of Britain and France and told his generals to withdraw if there was any opposition. But Britain and France did not want to risk war by opposing what Hitler had done. They protested, but took no action. This merely increased Hitler's confidence that he could do as he wanted without having to fear the consequences.

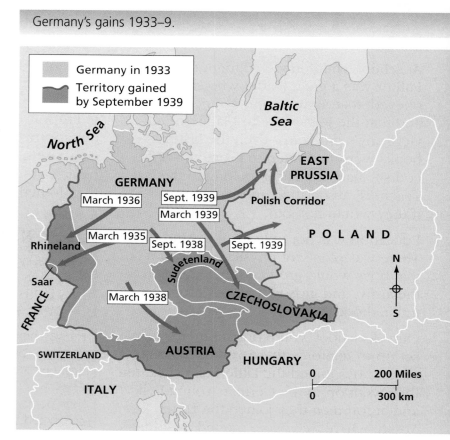

Germany's gains 1933–9.

- Germany in 1933
- Territory gained by September 1939

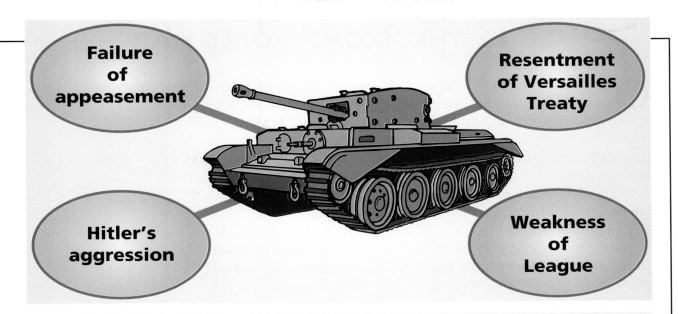

Reasons for the outbreak of war.

## Next stop Austria

Hitler was Austrian and longed to join the German-speaking country with Germany (although this was forbidden in the Treaty of Versailles).

In 1938 he instructed pro-German Austrians to start trouble in the country and then sent troops in to 'restore order'. The Austrian Chancellor resigned and Britain and France complained bitterly, but they were not prepared to take action. Britain preferred a policy of **appeasement** – preventing war by negotiation.

This policy was soon brought into action over Czechoslovakia. Hitler demanded that the Sudetenland area, where three million Germans lived, should be given to Germany. He threatened to invade if his wish was not granted. At a meeting in Munich in September 1938 Britain, France, Italy and Germany agreed that Germany should have the Sudetenland and Hitler said that he had no more land he wanted to gain. The British Prime Minister, Neville Chamberlain was given a hero's reception when he returned to London. He had saved Europe from war. The Czechs were disgusted and President Benes resigned in protest.

Six months later Chamberlain realised that he had been tricked when Hitler invaded and occupied the rest of Czechoslovakia. Both Britain and France stepped up the process of arming themselves for the war that now seemed inevitable. Since Poland looked like Hitler's next target (it had been formed in 1919 partly with land taken from Germany) the two countries agreed to help Poland if Hitler attacked.

Britain and France did not expect Hitler to attack Poland because the Soviet Union also wanted land there and would not let Hitler occupy the country. But in August 1939 Stalin and Hitler decided that for the moment it suited them to be allies. They signed the Nazi-Soviet Pact and agreed to share Poland between them. On 1 September Hitler invaded and two days later Britain and France declared war – though there was little they could do to save Poland.

### Neville Chamberlain (1869–1940)

Chamberlain is famous as the British Prime Minister who tried to avoid war by having direct one-to-one discussions with Hitler. Chamberlain abandoned this policy in 1939 and resigned after Hitler invaded Norway in 1940.

# 2.2 THE SECOND WORLD WAR

On 3 September 1939 Britain and Germany were again at war. Two days earlier German dive-bombers, low-flying fighter planes and armoured divisions smashed into Poland. This was Hitler's 'lightning war' or **blitzkrieg**. It worked against Poland and six months later Hitler struck again. Nazi troops overran Denmark, Norway, Holland and Belgium. On 12 May 1940, skirting round the old defences built since the war, German troops invaded France. The British Expeditionary Force, sent to help guard France's frontier with Belgium, was sliced in two. In the north, the BEF and French troops were trapped on the beach at Dunkirk. Hundreds of small boats, yachts and pleasure steamers heard about this and set out from Britain, and with the navy managed to rescue around 338,000 British and French soldiers from the beaches of Dunkirk. To the south, the Germans soon overran French forces, and on 22 June the French surrendered. From then until the end of the war, the Germans allowed the French to govern most of central and southern France from the town of Vichy, but the Vichy government was always under German control and influence.

After the fall of France, Britain stood alone against Nazi Germany and its allies (the Axis powers).

The war in Europe and North Africa, 1939–42.

Map legend:
- Neutral countries
- Axis powers and their allies
- Areas conquered by the Axis 1939–42 (with dates of conquest)
- Vichy France – ruled by the French under German influence

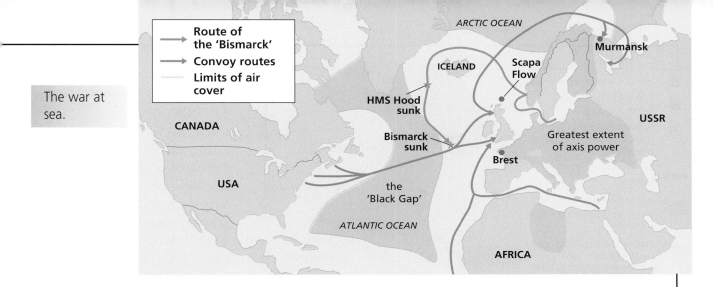

The war at sea.

## The war at sea

Britain's survival as a nation and as a fighting force depended upon keeping the sea routes open. Along these sea routes, food and raw materials were shipped to Britain, and Britain was able to help supply the Allies. The aim of the Germans was to sink as many ships steaming for Britain as possible and so starve the British into surrender.

Allied cargo ships travelled in **convoys** with British destroyers to protect them from German attacks. Food, petrol and aeroplanes were shipped across the Atlantic from the USA and, after the USA joined in the war, troops crossed too. Arctic convoys carried lorries, tanks and aeroplanes to Russia. Supplies for the British Eighth Army were shipped through the Mediterranean Sea.

After the fall of France in 1940, German ships, based in the French port of Brest, attacked Allied shipping deep in the Atlantic. The German battleship *Bismarck* tried to get to Brest from the Baltic Sea to join them but, after sinking the British battleship *HMS Hood*, was itself sunk by the British navy.

German submarines (U-boats), operating from French ports, attacked convoys crossing the Atlantic. These U-boats hunted in packs and were so successful that Churchill, Britain's leader, talked about the 'Battle of the Atlantic'. In March 1943 forty U-boats attacked two Allied convoys, consisting of ninety-two ships, in the 'Black Gap' beyond the range of aircraft cover. One U-boat and twenty-one Allied ships were sunk.

The development of sonar meant that submarines could be detected quickly and accurately, and the breaking of German secret codes began to turn the war at sea in the Allies' favour.

### Andrew Cunningham (1883–1963)

In 1939, Andrew Cunningham commanded the British naval forces in the Mediterranean. This was a key post, especially after 1940 when Italy entered the war on the side of Germany. He had to try to safeguard Allied shipping, which crossed Italian sea routes between Tripoli and the Italian navy bases at Taranto (1940) and Cape Matapan (1941). He was in command of Allied naval forces during the invasion of North Africa (1942) and Sicily and Italy (1942). In 1943 he was made Admiral of the Fleet and First Sea Lord. At the end of the war, he was made a viscount.

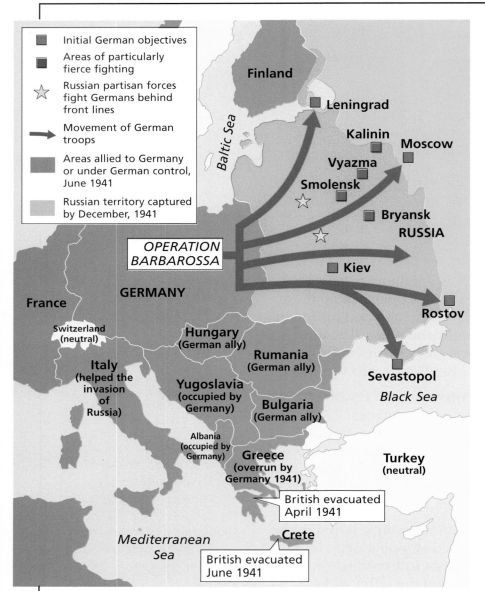

**Legend:**
- Initial German objectives
- Areas of particularly fierce fighting
- ⭐ Russian partisan forces fight Germans behind front lines
- ➜ Movement of German troops
- Areas allied to Germany or under German control, June 1941
- Russian territory captured by December, 1941

Finland

Baltic Sea

Leningrad

Kalinin

Moscow

Vyazma

Smolensk

Bryansk

RUSSIA

Kiev

Rostov

*OPERATION BARBAROSSA*

GERMANY

France

Switzerland (neutral)

Hungary (German ally)

Rumania (German ally)

Italy (helped the invasion of Russia)

Yugoslavia (occupied by Germany)

Bulgaria (German ally)

Albania (occupied by Germany)

Greece (overrun by Germany 1941)

Sevastopol

Black Sea

Turkey (neutral)

British evacuated April 1941

*Mediterranean Sea*

Crete

British evacuated June 1941

Operation Barbarossa.

## The war in eastern Europe

On 22 June 1941 Hitler launched 'Operation Barbarossa'. This was the invasion of Russia. He wanted to defeat communism and he wanted to find 'lebensraum' (living space) for the German people. This was probably Hitler's greatest mistake. In the end, campaigns over the vastness of Russia exhausted the German army.

At first the German 'blitzkrieg' was very successful and the Germans advanced deep into Russia. By the end of 1941 they had captured the Baltic countries and had laid siege to Leningrad (now called St Petersburg); they had reached the Black Sea, capturing the rich agricultural and industrial areas of the Ukraine on the way, and had reached the suburbs of Moscow.

What went wrong? German troops spent a terrible winter in Russia and it wasn't until June 1942 that they began to advance again. This time their aim was to capture Moscow and the oil-fields of the Caucasus. They were stopped at the city of Stalingrad (now called Volgograd). For five months the German army laid siege to the city. The Russians inside suffered dreadfully, and were reduced to eating stray cats and dogs as well as rats. Eventually Russian troops under their commander, Marshal Zhukov, surrounded the German army. In January 1943, 100,000 soldiers and 23 generals surrendered.

The Russians pushed the Germans back and back until, by the end of 1944, all Russian lands had been recaptured and the Russian armies were invading Germany.

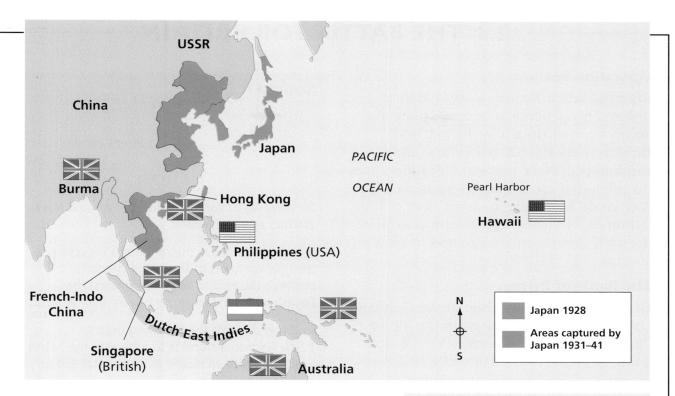

The expansion of Japan.

## The war in the Far East 1931–42

Japan was trying to create an empire in the Far East long before the Second World War broke out. By the beginning of 1941 the Japanese controlled large areas of eastern China. This was part of their plan, called the Greater East Asia Co-prosperity Sphere, by which they aimed to gain economic control of the Far East. But in their way stood the British Empire and the US navy.

In 1940, when Britain stood alone against Nazi Germany, the British Empire seemed to be collapsing. Certainly Great Britain, fighting for survival, was not able to send troops to defend Singapore or Burma. The USA was a different matter. Strong, and keeping out of the war, America greatly disapproved of Japan's military expansion, and might use its huge fleet, stationed in the Pacific at Pearl Harbor in the Hawaiian Islands, to oppose it. And Hitler had guaranteed to support Japan in the event of an Allied attack. Japan took a chance. Without warning, on Sunday 7 December 1941, 400 Japanese planes rained bombs and torpedoes onto the American fleet. They sank or severely damaged 18 warships and killed nearly 3000 people. Japan had entered the Second World War. But so, too, had America.

### Georgi Zhukov (1896–1974)

Georgi Zhukov was Commander-in-Chief of the Red Army from October 1941 until 1945.

Zhukov's parents were peasants. As a young man he worked as a furrier in Moscow. When the First World War broke out, he fought in the Tsar's army and, after 1918, in the Red Army. He became an expert in tank warfare. In December 1941, he ended the German siege of Moscow and two years later brought about the end of the siege of Stalingrad. At the end of the war he liberated Warsaw and led Russian troops into Berlin.

After the war, Zhukov became commander-in-chief of the Russian zone of Germany. He was made minister of defence in 1955. Two years later he was sacked and accused of making 'political mistakes' during the war.

## Operation Sealion

After the fall of France, in 1941 Hitler ordered his generals to prepare plans for an invasion of Britain. At French and Belgian ports 100,000 troops assembled. Landing craft were prepared. But there was no point in a cross-channel invasion if the RAF could bomb the invading fleet out of existence. Germany had to gain control of the air if Operation Sealion was to be a success.

## The Battle of Britain

Herman Goering, the chief of the German Luftwaffe (airforce) was given the job of destroying the RAF. It looked as if it was going to be easy. The Luftwaffe had 2670 planes and the RAF 600. The Luftwaffe, however, had more bombers than fighters, and their fighters could only operate for half an hour at a time, before they ran out of fuel. The RAF also had radar, which could pin-point the position of enemy planes and direct fighter squadrons accurately. The battle was not going to be easy.

On 15 August 1940 the Luftwaffe began an all-out effort to smash the RAF. For nearly a month the skies of southern England were filled with the vapour trails of battling aircraft. Airfields were bombed and hundreds of fighters shot down. By the beginning of September the RAF was dangerously short of planes and pilots. It was reckoned that the life expectancy of an RAF fighter pilot was just fourteen days.

Suddenly it stopped. German High Command had decided the Luftwaffe's losses were too great. The Luftwaffe turned to bombing Britain's cities and Hitler decided to try to invade Russia. Operation Sealion was called off.

### Source A

The orders sent by Hitler to the Luftwaffe.

**Führer's Headquarters**
**1 August 1940**
**TOP SECRET**

Directive No.17 for the Conduct of Air and Naval Warfare against England.

In order to establish the conditions necessary for the final conquest of England, I intend to continue the air and naval war against the English homeland more intensively than before.

To this end I issue the following orders:
1 The German airforce is to overcome the British airforce with all means at its disposal and as soon as possible.
2 Attacks on the harbours of the south coast are to be undertaken on the smallest scale possible, in view of our intended operations.
3 The Luftwaffe is to stand by in force for Operation Sealion.

**ADOLF HITLER**

All RAF pilots were men, but women also played their part in the Battle of Britain. In this painting a WAAF (Women's Auxiliary Air force) squad is raising a barrage balloon outside Coventry. Barrage balloons were attached to the ground by cables. If an enemy plane flew too low, it either hit the balloon or got entangled in the cables.

### Source B

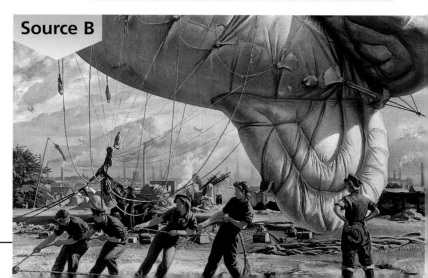

## Source C

An account of the first day of the Blitz in Stepney, in the East End of London – one of many reports collected by 'Mass Observation'.

**At 8.15 p.m. a colossal crash, as if the whole street was collapsing; the shelter itself is shaking. Immediately an ARP [Air Raid Precaution] helper, a nurse, begins singing lustily in an attempt to drown out the noise: 'Roll out the barrel' while Mrs S., wife of a dyer and cleaner, screams 'My house! It hit my house! My house is blown to bits!' As the bombing continues, a man shouts at the ARP helper who is still trying to get people to sing, 'Shut your bleedin' row!'**

### The Blitz

Once Hitler realised that he could not defeat the RAF, he tried to bomb the British into submission in the Blitz. From September 1940 to May 1941 bombs rained down on London and other major cities. Although London was the main target, ports and harbours, factories and homes throughout Britain were destroyed. This put tremendous pressure on the rescue, fire-fighting and ambulance services. Communal air-raid shelters were built at the end of streets; people had Anderson air-raid shelters, which were corrugated steel huts covered with earth, in their gardens. They had Morrison shelters, which were steel tables, inside their houses. Thousands of Londoners slept on Underground railway platforms. At night, people volunteered to 'fire watch'; street lights and car headlights were dimmed and every window had 'black-out' curtains, pulled so that not a chink of light could show. This 'black-out' made it difficult for German bombers to spot their targets. Sirens wailed when a raid was about to start so that people could take shelter.

Even so, by the end of May 1941, over 60,000 British people had been killed. Then Hitler turned his attention to Russia.

This photograph was taken in London during the Blitz.

## Radar

Radar stands for **ra**dio **d**etection **a**nd **r**anging. It worked by bouncing a radio wave against a distant object and picking up the returning radio wave as a blip on a screen. Operators could then work out how far away the object was and the speed and direction in which it was travelling.

In 1936 work started on a system of radar stations around the southern and eastern coasts of England. They were finished in time to be used during the Second World War. They gave British defences early warning of incoming enemy planes, whether they were bombers or fighters. Radar was also installed in ships and on planes.

# 2.4 BOMBS, BOMBS, BOMBS

## Why bomb?

Allied and Axis planes bombed cities. They bombed to destroy factories and docks, shipyards and railways. They bombed to create fear in ordinary people and destroy morale.

## Precision bombing

Some raids were made on military targets such as factories and shipyards. In 1943 Allied planes made a daring raid on the German rocket factory at Peenemunde. In the same year 'bouncing bombs', developed by Barnes Wallis, were used to damage the Mohne and Eder dams in the Ruhr.

However, it was difficult to hit targets accurately. Night flying was difficult unless there was a moon. Even then, cloud and smoke tended to blot out the targets, and fighter planes, barrage balloons, searchlights and anti-aircraft guns made the job even more difficult. It was easier to bomb in daylight – but it was easier for the fighters, too, to locate and bring down the bombers before they reached their targets. Before long, precision bombing was virtually abandoned. Airforce leaders began to think that, in total war, no distinction should be made between armed forces and civilians.

## Source B

Bombs dropped on Britain and Germany 1940–5.

| Year | Britain | Germany |
|------|---------|---------|
| 1940 | 37,000  | 10,000  |
| 1941 | 21,000  | 30,000  |
| 1942 | 3000    | 40,000  |
| 1943 | 9000    | 120,000 |
| 1944 | 2000    | 650,000 |
| 1945 | 750     | 500,000 |

## Source C

Written by Vera Brittain in 1943.

The change from the 'precision' bombing of military objectives to the present 'obliteration' bombing of whole areas with their churches, libraries, schools, hospitals, museums and vulnerable human beings came with the appointment of Sir Arthur Harris to the control of Bomber Command on 3 March 1942.

This is a policy of murder and massacre in the name of the British people.

Source A

"By the way, did you remember to feed the canary?"

This cartoon was published during the Second World War.

## Dresden 1945: necessity or revenge?

By the beginning of 1945 it was clear that the Allies would win the war. It was only a matter of time. In order to bring the war in Europe to a quick end, the Allies decided on 'Operation Thunderclap': a massive assault on civilian targets planned to break the morale of ordinary German people. The target chosen was Dresden, a beautiful medieval city that had never been bombed before. On the nights of 13 and 14 February the RAF and USAAF destroyed the city. Over 135,000 people died in a horrific firestorm, a far greater number than the 51,500 British civilians killed by the Luftwaffe during the whole of the war.

Dresden after the Allied raids of 1945.

### Source D

### Source E

Sir Arthur Harris, who was in charge of Bomber Command 1942–5, explains why he ordered the bombing of Dresden.

**Dresden had by this time become the main centre of communications for the defence of Germany. It was also by far the largest city in Germany which had been left intact; it had never been bombed. As a large centre of war industry it was also of the highest importance.**

### Source F

From a radio broadcast by the official German foreign information services.

**The Americans have proved that they can hit precise targets whenever they please. It would therefore have been possible to have spared the residential districts of Dresden and the historic town centre. The use of incendiaries (fire bombs) proves that residential districts were being deliberately attacked. It is pointless to drop incendiaries on railways.**

### Arthur Harris (1892–1984)

Sir Arthur Harris, (nicknamed 'Bomber' Harris) was Commander-in-Chief of Bomber Command from 1942. He concentrated on area bombing of the enemy and aimed to destroy housing, break morale and damage industrial production. Beautiful cities were destroyed, civilians were killed and many RAF bomber crews were shot down during these raids.

Churchill, the British Prime Minister, supported Harris' plans. However, after the bombing of Nuremberg in March 1944 and Dresden in February 1945, more and more people, including other RAF commanders, said that area bombing could not be defended on moral grounds.

After the war, Harris was the only senior commander not to be offered a peerage. A statue to him was not put up until 1992 and when it was unveiled, people in the crowd jeered and booed.

## What was evacuation?

The British government made plans to send children from cities to live in the countryside where they would be safe. In London, the plans were put into operation on 1 September 1939 and within four days over one million children were sent to the West Country and to Wales. But because the bombs didn't fall immediately, parents gradually took their children back home. There was another wave of evacuation in 1940 when the Blitz began, and again in 1944 when Germany began launching the V1 and V2 'flying bombs'.

## How did evacuation work?

Mothers usually went with children under school age, but most children went alone or with their brothers and sisters. Sometimes teachers would go with the children in their class. The children had a label tied on them giving their name and home address. They could take one suitcase and had to have their gas mask with them. Parents did not always know where their children were going when they set off. They just had to believe government promises that their children would be well looked after.

The children were **billeted** with families who had room for them. The government paid families 10s 6d a week for the first child billeted and 8s 6d a week each for any others. Not all the families wanted children from the big cities staying with them, and not all the children wanted to live away from home. Some children settled in well, others were desperately unhappy.

**Source A**

Children walking to Blackhouse Road station, north-east London, in 1939 to be evacuated.

## Source B

Beryl Hewitson describes what happened to her when she arrived in the country.

We were told to sit quietly on the floor while villagers and farmers' wives came to choose which children they wanted. Eventually only my friend Nancy and myself were left – two plain, straight-haired little girls wearing glasses, now rather tearful. A large, happy-looking, middle-aged lady rushed in asking, 'Is that all you have left?' A sad, slow nod of the head from our teacher. 'I'll take the poor bairns.' We were led out of the hall with this stranger and taken to a farm where we spent two years.

## Source C

Patricia Barton remembers life as an evacuee.

The village didn't know what hit them when we first arrived. It was gang warfare between us and the local kids. There wasn't a fruit tree within miles around with a single item of fruit left on it. After a while things settled down to an uneasy truce.

## Source D

Extracts from reports sent to the Women's Institute Headquarters in 1940.

The children were filthy; we have never seen so many children with lice and nits lacking any knowledge of clean and hygienic habits. It seemed they hadn't bathed for months; some children had dirty, septic sores all over their bodies. Some of the children were sewn into their ragged little garments. There was hardly a child with a whole pair of shoes. Many of the mothers and children were bedwetters and were not in the habit of doing anything else.

## Source E

Chris Portinari had three homes as an evacuee. He was sent away from the first because he helped himself to sugar. Two boys in the second home bullied him very badly.

They would tie me to a chair and held red-hot pokers in front of my eyes. I had terrible nightmares. I was sent away when the three of us took down the knickers of the girl next door. I ended up in a spick and span place. Every day I would come home from school to 'Clean this, shine that.' So I started to save my milk money, a halfpenny a day. I came home one day and wrote across the list of things to do, 'GONE BACK TO LONDON'. My mother hid me in the attic for two days before telling my father. I wasn't sent back and stayed in London during the raids.

Some women looked after many evacuee children! They could be awarded the British Empire Medal for doing this.

## Source F

## Source G

Sheila Price was the second of eight children from Hammersmith, London. She was evacuated when she was twelve years old.

The orchard bore fruit, we had a car to take us to school, a piano, a beautiful home, servants, typing lessons, mini-golf and a fine lawn. Most of all we met warmth and understanding.

I became a snob. Each weekend I'd board the bus home. The street looked dingy, poor – I hated it. I remember seeing my father cooking a pigeon on our kitchen fire and the repulsion stayed with me. Eventually Mother called me home to look after the others. Then my lovely world crumbled.

## V1s and V2s

The second 'wave' of evacuation happened in 1944 when Germany began attacking Britain with 'flying bombs' – the V1s and V2s.

The V1 was a plane without a pilot. Loaded with explosives, it simply crashed when its fuel ran out. People on the ground close to a V1 could hear its engine cut out when the fuel was used up. They then had to wait in the terrifying silence until it hit the ground and exploded. The first V1 fell on 15 June 1944. V1s were aimed at London and south-east England. People called them 'doodle-bugs' or 'buzz-bombs.' They killed over 6000 people until Allied armies, invading Germany, overran their launching sites.

Germany launched the first V2 against Britain in September 1944 and the last in March 1945. V2s were liquid fuelled, radio-guided rockets, which travelled at supersonic speed. The most frightening thing about them was that they were silent. No one had any warning until there was a tremendous explosion – and then it was too late. V2s killed nearly 3000 people.

Winnie Farley married Leslie Williams in 1938. War was declared the following year, and Leslie volunteered to fight. He joined the Royal Engineers and in February 1941 was sent abroad to Africa and then the Middle East. Five months later, Winnie and Leslie's daughter Margaret was born. Leslie didn't see her until she was four years old.

Here Winnie remembers her war.

### Keeping in touch

*I never really knew where Leslie was. We wives weren't supposed to, but sometimes he would be able to write that he had had some leave in Alexandria, or Gaza, so I knew he was still in the Middle East. I sent him parcels. He always wanted Keatings Powders to kill the lice and bed bugs. I knitted mittens and socks and woollen caps. When I could get eggs and fat I baked cakes for him and sent them out in tins. He always wanted soap, too, especially shaving soap. Everything took such a long time. It was three weeks before he got the news that Margaret had been born.*

A photograph of Leslie, taken during the war.

**Source A**

### War work

*Before Margaret was born I worked in Chichester as a nurse with the VADs [Voluntary Aid Detachment]. I nursed soldiers and civilians. In 1940, after Dunkirk, we all thought Hitler was going to invade and the south coast was a dangerous place to be. The civilian patients were all taken somewhere safer and we were left with the soldiers. For some reason I wasn't thought good enough to nurse soldiers so I was sent to nurse people who were mentally disturbed. Every door had to be locked and unlocked. As well as having a huge bunch of keys, I also carried a whistle which I had to blow if there was trouble. I'll always remember Georgie. She would go to sleep sitting bolt upright and with her eyes wide open. She pushed a wicker chair everywhere she went, even to the loo.*

### Air raids and eiderdowns

*When I was at home in Chichester and the sirens went, I would take the baby into bed with me and pull the eiderdown over both of us. An ATS officer was billeted with us and she used to come under the eiderdown too! She said she wasn't afraid – she just couldn't stop shaking.*

### Fish and blackcurrants

*Fish wasn't rationed, but there wasn't much of it. I queued for hours for a piece of plaice for Margaret. And then she would only eat it if it was covered with blackcurrant purée. What a waste of good fish! And I had queued for so long for it!*

## Air raids and shelters

*We had a Sussex spaniel called Nobby who came with us when we visited my parents in Croydon. If there was an air raid, he rushed out of the house and was waiting by the shelter door almost before the sirens had stopped. He was always the first out of the shelter when the 'All clear' sounded.*

## Butter

*Butter was rationed – sometimes to only 2oz a week. I used to pour the top of the milk into a small jar and screwed the top on tightly. Then I shook and shook the jar until the milk turned to butter.*

## Children's parties

*My friend Joan was upset because she hadn't any eggs and so couldn't make a cake for Paul's third birthday. So I made it for her, and instead of eggs I used liquid paraffin. It worked beautifully: the cake rose well and was very tasty.*

*A woman we knew asked us to bring our children to a party. You never saw such food! There were scones thick with butter, iced cakes and chocolate biscuits. She must have got it all on the* **black market**. *We always wondered what she did to get it!*

A photograph of Winnie and Margaret, taken during the war.

**Source B**

## Sausages and ham

*We were only allowed 4oz [113 grams] of meat a week, but sausages, when you could get them, weren't rationed. Our butcher sold sausage 'sandwiches'. He put a slice of sausage meat in between two slices of potato and dipped the whole thing in dried milk and breadcrumbs. They were really quite tasty. Sometimes I managed to get a ham knuckle with a bit of meat left on it. I shaved off the bits of ham and cooked them with potatoes and herbs. The ham bone I boiled up with split peas to make a good soup.*

## Call-up

In 1939, Parliament passed the National Service Act. All fit men aged 18–41 had to register for military service. A man could say whether he wanted to join the navy, the air force or the army. Most ended up in the army. If a man was doing work that was important to the war effort, such as mining, he didn't have to join the armed forces. Altogether, throughout the war, nearly 8.5 million men registered. Of these, 60,000 were conscientious objectors: men who believed it was morally wrong to fight.

## Eggs and hens

*Eggs were rationed to one a week and sometimes one every two weeks. An old lady in the next village kept hens and used to let me have eggs for Margaret. Then the men from the ministry caught up with her and she had to stop. So she gave me two hens which she said had stopped laying. But they laid two eggs a day for me all through the war, except on Sundays when they only managed one.*

# 2.7 THE SECRET ARMIES: THE RESISTANCE MOVEMENTS IN OCCUPIED EUROPE

By 1942 Hitler controlled most of Europe. (Look back at the map on page 34 to remind yourself of which these countries were.) Each country became a **police state**, with a governor and an army of occupation. People living in these countries had a difficult choice. They could **collaborate** with the enemy. They could join a resistance movement, which was dangerous because if they were caught they could expect no mercy. Or they could try to get on with their lives as best they could. This was what most people did. But in every occupied country there were people resisting the enemy occupiers.

## The French Resistance

One of the most famous resistance groups was the French Maquis. School children and milkmen, mayors and plumbers, café owners and teachers all tried in their own ways to undermine the German occupation.

The French Maquis hid Allied airmen who had been shot down and organised escape routes for them. They blew up bridges and railway lines. They made contact with the Free French forces in exile in Britain and their leader, Charles de Gaulle.

The Germans wreaked terrible revenge on any Maquis they caught. They destroyed the village of Oradour-sur-Glane and killed all the men, women and children living there because of the activities of local resistance groups. Later they discovered they had got the wrong village. By 1944 the Maquis were openly fighting the Germans and sending intelligence reports to Britain to help with the D-Day landings.

## Source A

From a book called *Maquis* by G. Millar published in 1945.

**For supplies we relied on Paincheau. We needed petrol. The Germans kept it in tanks in a guarded building. One night they parked a tanker beside a wall of the building that was not guarded. One man, a stonemason, silently cut a hole in the wall. His comrades ran a pipe through to the tank and all night pumped out petrol. The mason then rebuilt the wall. They did the same thing the next night. Finally, before the Germans noticed the levels going down, Paincheau's men put 200 kilos of sugar in the tank. [Sugar dissolves in petrol, so the Germans would not know it was there until they filled their vehicles with the petrol. The sugar in the petrol would then ruin the engines.]**

## Source B

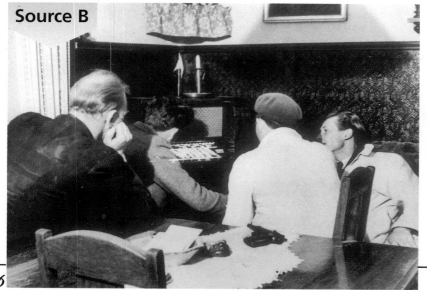

In this photograph Danish resistance workers from Odense listen to a radio broadcast from London in 1945. If they had been caught, the Nazis would have killed them. The BBC broadcast coded instructions to resistance workers; it broadcast news of the war, which was different from the Nazi version; and it broadcast the first bars from Beethoven's 5th symphony. Listen to them. They sound just like the Morse Code for 'V' (which is dot, dot, dot, dash). V for victory, of course.

## The Netherlands

The Resistance flourished in the Netherlands, in spite of Seyss-Inquart, the Reichskommissar for the Netherlands. He was hated by the Dutch because of his brutal regime. The Dutch Resistance ran underground newspapers which spread information. German offices were blown up and leading Nazis were assassinated. Although the Nazis sent five million Dutch workers to Germany, the Resistance hid 300,000 runaways and gave them false papers. Many families hid Jews to prevent their deportation. Even so, around 104,000 out of 140,000 Dutch Jews died in Nazi concentration camps.

## Source C

In 1942 Anne Frank, her parents and sister Margot, together with four other Jews, went into hiding in a secret annexe in Otto Frank's office. Loyal friends kept them supplied and kept them safe. Anne kept a diary.

*11 July 1942* **We've forbidden Margot to cough even though she has a bad cold, and are giving her large doses of codeine.**

*24 December 1943* **Whenever someone comes in from outside, with the wind in their clothes and the cold on their cheeks, I feel like burying my head under the blankets to keep from thinking 'When will we be allowed to breathe fresh air again?'**

*3 April 1944* **The high point is our weekly slice of liver sausage, and jam on our unbuttered bread. But we're still alive!**

*21 July 1944* **I'm finally getting optimistic. Now, at last, things are going well! They really are! Great news! An assassination attempt has been made on Hitler's life. The prospect of going back to school in October is making me too happy!**

Someone tipped off the Gestapo. On 4 August 1944 they arrested Anne and her family. Her mother died of hunger and exhaustion in the Auschwitz concentration camp on 6 January 1945. Margot and Anne were moved from Auschwitz to the Bergen-Belsen concentration camp. There they died from typhus sometime in February or March 1945. The Allies liberated Belsen on 12 April 1945. Their father, Otto, survived until 1980.

**Source D**

Large resistance groups operated in Nazi-occupied parts of the Soviet Union. They formed partisan armies – armed civilians who fought occupying troops. These Russians are being hanged by the Germans because they were partisans.

## White Rose

The White Rose movement was a resistance movement organised by young people in Germany. It operated between 1939 and early 1943. Based in Munich University, it was run by Hans and Sophie Scholl.

When it was first formed, the White Rose movement concentrated on printing and distributing anti-Nazi material around the university. Then the Scholls expanded their activities. They began collecting information about the terrible things the Nazi regime was doing. They did not stop there. They spread this information around the main towns in central Germany. Then, in early 1943, the Scholls stopped being secretive about what they were doing. They began openly to distribute anti-Nazi propaganda. They were arrested immediately, tried and found guilty. In February 1943, they were executed in Stadelheim prison.

# 2.8  THE SECRET ARMIES: THE SPECIAL OPERATIONS EXECUTIVE

The British realised that resistance groups in occupied Europe were helping to sabotage the German war effort and could supply the Allies with useful information. In July 1940 Winston Churchill, Britain's Prime Minister, set up the Special Operations Executive (SOE) to, as he said, *co-ordinate all action by way of **subversion** and sabotage against the enemy overseas.* France had fallen and Britain was, then, the only European country to stand against Nazi Germany. The RAF, after the Battle of Britain and the Blitz, was too weak for an immediate air strike on Germany. So Britain sent small raiding parties along the coasts of Europe and parachuted secret agents behind enemy lines. These secret agents worked with, and sometimes helped to set up, local resistance groups.

SOE agents went to the Balkans, the Baltic, Italy, Scandinavia, the Netherlands, Belgium, France and central Europe. Their success depended largely on local politics and geography. They could not, for example, stop the Nazis penetrating the Dutch Resistance, which led to the deaths of over 20,000 people. On the other hand, the SOE worked successfully with Yugoslavian partisans fighting German troops in the mountains. However, most SOE agents worked in France, where almost 200 of them were executed. In 1945 only 30 agents survived.

## Source A

This canister is going to be dropped behind enemy lines in France. It contains equipment for the Maquis.

## Source B

Major-General Sir Colin Gubbins, Head of the SOE.

**All contacts with occupied countries closed when the last British forces returned to Great Britain in 1940, so the first man to go back to any country had to be parachuted 'blind'. There was no one waiting to receive him on the dropping ground, no household ready to give him shelter, conceal his kit and arrange his onward passage.**

## Source C

An aircraft carrying SOE agents and drops SOE equipment for agents on the ground.

## VIOLETTE SZABO

Violette's father was an English soldier who met and married her mother in France at the end of the First World War. Violette spent her childhood in Brixton, London and worked in Woolworth's when she left school. She married a Free French soldier and because she spoke fluent French worked for the SOE. She was parachuted into France many times and in the 1950s her story was made into a film *Carve Her Name with Pride*. This is the story of her last mission.

It was just before D-Day and Violette was parachuted into France to take charge of a Maquis unit. Things went badly wrong. Violette and the local Maquis leader were ambushed by an SS Unit trying to get to Normandy and the D-Day beaches. Injured, Violette urged the Maquis leader to get away. He had more important things to do than save her life. She took cover behind some trees in a cornfield and for two hours held off 400 Germans and two tanks. Finally she ran out of ammunition and was captured. The Maquis planned her rescue but she was moved unexpectedly to Paris. Then, in August 1944 Violette was sent to Ravensbruck, an enormous concentration camp for women. There, on 26 January 1945, when the Allies were invading Germany and the war in France was over, she was condemned to death, shot in the neck from behind, and cremated.

## HARRY RÉE (HENRI)

Harry Rée was a graduate of Cambridge University and a school teacher when he joined the SOE. He parachuted into France many times, set up and ran resistance networks, killed and sabotaged. He was never caught. This is the story of one of his exploits.

Captain Harry Rée.

The great Peugeot car works at Sochaux was making gun-carriers and gun turrets for German Panzers. The RAF had not been able to do more than damage it. Harry was asked to destroy the works from inside, by sabotage. Monsieur Sire, the personnel manager at the works, secretly supported the Resistance. He gave Harry a pass and arranged for him to see Rudolphe Peugeot, the boss. Monsieur Peugeot gave Harry the factory plans. He helped him select the points where the explosives should be placed and introduced him to two trustworthy factory foremen. Harry arranged for explosives to be smuggled inside the factory and hidden in a cleaner's cupboard. On the chosen night, the foremen, avoiding the sentries, placed the charges in the transformer hall, the assembly plant and the steel presses and escaped through the nightwatchman's room. At ten minutes past midnight the works blew up. Within minutes SS and army units arrived and cordoned off the whole area. The next morning Sochaux was swarming with the dreaded Gestapo. No one was caught.

## *Concentration camps*

Ravensbruck, to which Violette Szabo (above) was sent, was an all-female concentration camp. Like Buchenwald, Sachsenhausen, Flossenburg and Mauthausen, it was set up before the war.

The first inmates of the camps were political opponents of the Nazi regime. Later, they were joined by anyone the Nazis thought were unfit for civilised society, including criminals, the homeless, gypsies, homosexuals, prostitutes, Jehovah's witnesses and Jews.

Each inmate was given a number, worn on a patch sewn to their clothes. They also wore a colour-coded triangle: red for political prisoners, pink for homosexuals and black for others. Jews wore a yellow triangle as part of a Star of David.

War brought huge numbers of new prisoners to the camps, including members of the resistance organisations in occupied Europe.

## What was it like to live in occupied Europe?

Most people in occupied Europe tried to get on with their everyday lives as best they could. But what was life like for them?

The economies of these countries were adjusted to serve the needs of Germany. Firms were taken over and raw materials and fuel used for German projects. Thousands of workers were sent to Germany to help with the German war effort. Banks were also taken over and German gold reserves grew. Everything cost more.

There were hundreds of everyday reminders of the Nazi take-over. German soldiers patrolled the streets, ate and drank in the cafés and bars. They took what they wanted, whether it was art treasures or girlfriends.

Some people decided they could survive best by working with the Nazi invaders. At the end of the war they paid a terrible price for this collaboration.

**Source A**

The woman with the shaved head was said to have had her baby by a German soldier. Now, carrying her baby, she is jeered and shouted at by the people where she lives. This photograph was taken in 1945 after the Germans had left France.

### VIDKUN QUISLING (1887–1945)

Quisling was a Norwegian diplomat. In the 1920s he worked for the League of Nations. From 1931 to 1933 he was Defence Minister in Norway. In 1933, when Hitler came to power in Germany, he founded the *Nasjonal Samlung* (National Party) which was really an imitation of Hitler's Nazi Party. In April 1940 the German army and air force began a massive assault on Norway. King Haakon and his government tried desperately to organise resistance. However, the Norwegian army was no match for the highly organised, efficient German war machine and, despite support from the RAF and the Royal Navy, Norway surrendered. The King and his government fled to Britain where they formed a Norwegian government-in-exile.

Vidkun Quisling stayed in Norway. The Nazis banned all political parties except the *Nasjonal Samlung* and Quisling became Prime Minister. He ran Norway just as the Nazis wanted, which was not, of course, how the Norwegian government-in-exile wanted things done. When Norway was liberated in May 1945, Quisling gave himself up to the Norwegian police. Evidence was produced at his trial which proved he was in regular and secret contact with the Nazis before the war, urging them to invade Norway. He was found guilty of high treason and shot by a firing squad.

His treachery was thought to be so dreadful that the word 'quisling' has come to mean 'traitor'.

## WILLIAM JOYCE (1906–46)

Britain's most famous traitor was William Joyce. Born in New York, he had Irish parents who took him to Ireland, where they lived until he was sixteen. In 1922 they emigrated to England and William Joyce joined the British Union of Fascists. He fled to Germany before war broke out. Between September 1939 and April 1945, Joyce broadcast to the British people from *Radio Hamburg*. His broadcasts were streams of propaganda and hatred. He told of villages and towns that would be bombed, of ships that would be sunk and of invasion plans. He also needled the British about food prices and censorship. British people became used to turning on their radios and hearing his posh voice saying 'Germany calling; Germany calling', and nicknamed him 'Lord Haw-Haw'. Eventually most people learned to laugh at him, but they still worried that what he said might be right. British troops captured Joyce near the Danish/German frontier and brought him back to Britain. Accused of treason, he was found guilty at the Old Bailey and later hanged.

## HENRI PHILIPPE PÉTAIN (1856–1951)

Pétain was a French soldier and politician. When he was a junior officer his confidential report said 'If this officer rises above the rank of major, it will be a disaster for France.' By 1917 he was Commander-in-Chief of the French army and revered as a war hero and saviour of his country.

Pétain was 84 when German troops began their advance through Belgium in 1939. The French government asked him to join them because it needed his advice. He said the government should not consider a military alliance with Great Britain. Once Germany had invaded France and occupied Paris, Pétain said that the French government should not carry on fighting, but should ask for an **armistice**. The Germans divided France into two zones: the north (occupied) and the south (unoccupied). Pétain led the government of the unoccupied south of France from the city of Vichy. He ran unoccupied France as the Germans wanted him to. The only thing he refused to do was to allow France to fight Britain. He dreamed of a state based on 'work, family and fatherland', which was very close to the Nazi idea of what a state should be. He abolished trade unions, set up official state youth organisations and allowed only one political party. Vichy France had an anti-Jewish policy and was nothing like the sort of France for which the Free French were fighting. Pétain was arrested when the Allies liberated France in 1944. He was accused of treason, tried and found guilty. Because of his age he was not executed but sentenced to life imprisonment.

### Pierre Laval (1883–1945)

Pierre Laval was Marshal Petain's deputy and rival when the Vichy government was set up in France in 1940. In 1942, the Nazis made him Prime Minister and he openly worked with them to introduce and support Nazi policies.

Many French people began to hate him when they realised he had agreed to ship French men and women to Germany so that they could work in Nazi factories to help the German war-effort.

After the war he was taken to Germany but he escaped to Spain. Spanish authorities returned him to France where he was tried for treason. He was found guilty and executed by firing squad in October 1945.

# 2.10 SECRETS AND SPIES

All countries need spies in wartime to tell them of enemy plans for battles. All countries need to keep secrets, too. War Offices need to send orders to army, navy and air force commanders without the enemy listening to them.

Governments do not always tell the truth to their own people about the way the war is going. They need to keep their people at home believing that all is going well: that the war will be won.

## Source B

you never know who's listening!

## CARELESS TALK COSTS LIVES

In Britain a whole series of posters warned people about the dangers of gossiping.

This photograph shows rescue workers searching for survivors in a bombed-out school. It is dated 20 January 1943 and was marked 'banned'.

## Source A

## Source C

This poster was designed to make people see that what they may regard as a nuisance (petrol going up in price) was nothing compared to the hardships suffered by merchant seamen. It was very nearly banned because the censor thought it would discourage men from joining the navy.

**"The price of petrol has been increased by one penny" – Official**

## The Enigma machine

Commanders usually communicated with their troops by radio. The problem was that they could never be sure whether or not the enemy was listening in. The Germans solved the problem by inventing the 'Enigma' machine. This 'scrambled' straightforward messages into code which no one could understand unless they had an up-to-date code book. To make things even more difficult, Enigma was automatically adjusted minute by minute. The British government set up a 'Codes and Cyphers School' at Bletchley Park in Buckinghamshire. Details about Enigma were passed on to the British by a Polish worker in the factory where they were made. Eventually the Enigma code was broken, but the British government kept this a secret. They let the Germans believe they were still trying – and listened in to all the messages sent via Enigma.

## The man who never was

In 1943 British Intelligence dressed a dead man in a Royal Marine's uniform and put false papers in his pockets. They chained a briefcase full of invasion plans to his wrist. Then they floated him in the sea off the coast of Spain. When the body was washed ashore, German agents quickly got hold of the papers in the man's briefcase. They were detailed invasion plans – but for the south coast of France, not the Normandy beaches where the Allies really planned to stage their come-back in Europe.

## RUDOLF ROSSLER

Rudolf Rossler was one of the most successful spies of the Second World War. He was a German and in 1933, when Hitler came to power, Rossler went to live in Lucerne, Switzerland. There he joined a Russian spy-ring and was given the code-name 'Lucy'.

Rossler kept in contact with his friends in Germany. Many of them became high-ranking officers in the army and navy and influential Nazis. Without realising it, they gave him a lot of highly secret information. He was able to tell the Allies about Germany's plans to attack Poland, Denmark and Norway; he warned the Russians about Operation Barbarossa and about German preparations for an attack on the Russians at Kursk in 1943.

The 'Lucy Ring' was never broken and was one of the best wartime spy rings.

**Source D**

An Enigma machine.

## Magic

This was the code-name for an American operation, set up in 1939, to break Japanese diplomatic and military codes.

Their first job was to break the 'Purple' code. A new cipher machine had been invented by Captain Jinsaburo Ito. After nineteen months it was finally cracked by Colonel William Friedman, who had a nervous breakdown as a result of stress.

The Americans were able to penetrate deeply into Japanese diplomatic communications. But, because there was no central system for passing on the decoded information, no one was alerted to the proposed Japanese attack on Pearl Harbor.

## Over here!

On 26 January 1942 American troops began to arrive in Britain. By May 1944 there were 1,526,965 Americans soldiers, sailors and airmen stationed in the UK, ready to take part in an Allied invasion of Hitler's Europe. These troops (called GIs because their uniform was supposed to be stamped 'General Issue'), were well-fed, well-dressed and well-paid, and they had a huge impact on the British people with whom they came into contact.

## The USAAF

By far the biggest impact was made by the USAAF (United States Army Air Forces) who were stationed throughout Britain and who became involved with local people in the towns and villages near to their bases. Although most GIs were stationed in East Anglia, there were many elsewhere in England and in Wales, Scotland and Northern Ireland.

## Non-combat troops

As well as combat troops, there were GIs who were responsible for supplying vehicles and planes, uniforms, food, guns,

### Source B

A woman who was a teenager during the Second World War remembers:

**Americans were 'cheeky' compared to our usual 'Mr Frigidaire Englishman', but what a boost to her ego when one is greeted with 'Hello Duchess!' (and you were treated like one!) or 'Hi, beautiful!' That was so GOOD! As we got to know these boys, how generous they were; we never lacked for chocolates or cigarettes or even precious luxuries like nylons that they could get for us.**

tanks, ammunition and everything a fighting force needed in order to operate efficiently. This sort of back-up is called 'supply and maintenance'.

## Marrying local girls

The two major US supply bases were in the north-west of England, at Burtonwood and Warton in Lancashire, which together housed 33,000 men by 1945. These men stayed on the same base all the time and had time off in nearby towns including Preston, Manchester and Liverpool. From Burtonwood alone, 7000 men married local girls between 1942 and 1993 when the base closed. During the Second World War there were 75,000 GI brides in Britain – and most of them eventually left their family and friends and went to join their new husbands in the USA.

Apart from this very obvious impact, the American GIs affected British people's language, their music and their general idea of how to have fun.

### Source A

Children stop an American GI to ask 'Have you any gum, chum?' They often did and gave it away freely. Sometimes the chewing gum became a currency, to be paid for going on errands to buy fish and chips or to fix a date with a boy's sister.

## Source C

A GI from Virginia remembers being invited home by a girl he met at a dance:

**We had a meal which even by American standards was great – complete with ham and much more. Only afterwards did I discover that I had eaten the family's rations for a month. So I soon corrected that. I went to see our Mess Sergeant and the next time I turned up at this girl's home, it was as if I was Santa Claus. I brought a large can of pears and a pork loin – and a lot more stuff.**

British families were encouraged to entertain GIs. It was soon ruled that GIs should take special rations with them for each day's stay: fruit or tomato juice, evaporated milk, peas, bacon, sugar, coffee, lard, butter and rice.

GI wives and babies wave goodbye to England from SS *Argentina*, one of the first ships to take the GI brides to the USA, on 26 January 1946. The youngest bride was 15 and the oldest 44. It was difficult for the GI brides to get to the USA after the war: the American government insisted that shipping the troops back took priority.

## Source D

British girls dance with GIs at an American base.

## Source E

## GI Bill of Rights

This important law gave special rights to GIs returning to the USA after the war. It said they were to have special education and training opportunities, government - guaranteed life insurance, medical care, pension rights and low rate loans for them to buy homes or farms.

By 1955, nearly four million former GIs had taken out special home loans. Nearly seven million had taken the education and training opportunities, including 250,000 black people who went to college for the first time.

This law gave millions of Americans, especially those from the working classes, opportunities to own their own homes and businesses that they would not otherwise have had.

By the end of April 1945 Germany was on the point of defeat. On 1 May Admiral Doenitz announced *our Führer, Adolf Hitler, has fallen. At the end of his struggle he met a hero's death.* In reality Hitler and his wife, Eva Braun, had both committed suicide in Hitler's bunker, deep under Berlin – though their bodies were never found. Hitler's death left Admiral Doenitz in charge and on 7 May he bowed to the inevitable and surrendered to the Allies. The war in the west was over. But what was to happen to Germany?

## Another settlement

The harsh settlement imposed in the Treaty of Versailles at the end of the First World War was a major cause of the Second World War. The Germans felt that they had been unfairly blamed for causing the war. It was important to behave differently now the Second World War was over.

Germany was badly in need of help. Allied bombers had reduced many cities to little more than rubble and millions of people were desperate for proper food, clothing and shelter.

To add to the problems, hundreds of thousands of German refugees had fled from eastern Germany into Berlin. They knew the Soviet Red Army, advancing on Berlin from the east, was carrying out terrible acts of revenge for the atrocities committed by German troops in the Soviet Union. The refugees were fleeing west to avoid this.

On 25 April the Soviet forces met up with troops from Britain, France and the USA, in Berlin. Germany was occupied by the armies of the four major Allies. What would happen now?

## The agreement

The Allied leaders had already given considerable thought to what should happen to Germany once the war was over. Roosevelt, Stalin and Churchill had met at Yalta in February 1945 and agreed that:

- Germany should be divided into four occupation zones, one controlled by Britain, one by the USA, one by France and one by the Soviet Union. The German capital, Berlin, would be divided in a similar way. This was to be a temporary solution until Germany recovered from the war.

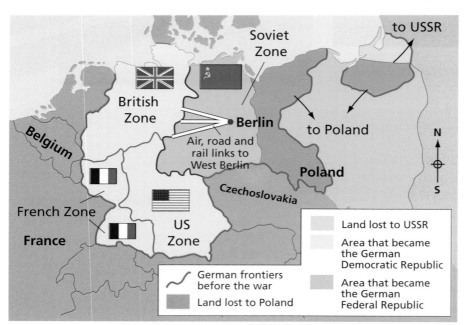

The division of Germany after the Second World War.

- The Allies would take goods and machinery from Germany as reparations for the cost of the war. So the Soviet Union began dismantling factories in its area of occupation and sending the equipment back to the Soviet Union.
- The countries that had been liberated from German occupation in eastern Europe would be allowed to have free elections to set up their own governments.

### Not according to plan

Unfortunately things did not work out as planned. The Soviet Union was determined to see communist governments elected in eastern Europe, to provide 'friendly' nations between it and the West. This resulted in the setting up of what Churchill called the 'Iron Curtain' dividing communist eastern Europe from democratic western Europe. The zones of occupation stayed and in 1949 the British, French and American zones became the German Federal Republic (West Germany). The Soviet zone became the German Democratic Republic (East Germany). Berlin, which was in the Soviet zone, remained divided into four zones and in 1961 the Soviet Union built the Berlin Wall to stop Berliners crossing from one zone to another.

So the map of Europe had been redrawn between the communist East and democratic West. Each side now lined up on either side of the Iron Curtain to fight the 'Cold War' (see pages 68–9). It was only when that dispute ended in 1990 that the two Germanies were finally re-united.

(see pages 68–9)

## Source A

Part of a speech made by ex-Prime Minister, Winston Churchill, in America in March 1946.

**A shadow has fallen across the scenes so lately lighted by Allied victory. From Stettin in the Baltic to Trieste in the Adriatic an Iron Curtain has descended across the continent.**

## Source B

A German soldier sits amongst the rubble of Berlin at the end of the war.

### Winston Churchill (1874–1965)

Churchill was the grandson of the Duke of Marlborough and was elected as a Conservative MP in 1900. Although he was held partly to blame for the disastrous Gallipoli campaign in the First World War, he was a brilliant war-time Prime Minister during the Second World War. He had always said that appeasement was wrong and took over when Chamberlain resigned in May 1940 (see page 33).

(see page 33)

## Japan on the advance

When the Japanese bombed Pearl Harbor on 7 December 1941 they caused enormous damage to the US Pacific fleet. It was to be some time before that fleet was rebuilt. In the meantime the Japanese took full advantage of the situation. They knew that the European powers with territories in South-East Asia were fighting a war of survival against Hitler's Germany. They could not spare the necessary men and equipment to defend their colonies. With the American fleet out of action there was little to stop the highly trained Japanese forces from taking control of vast areas of South-East Asia. Within six months of the bombing of Pearl Harbor, the Japanese had captured European bases stretching from Hong Kong in the north to Java in the south.

Britain's supposedly impregnable fortress at Singapore had been captured with ease, and 80,000 men taken prisoner of war. Even India and Australia looked threatened.

## Japan: 'Liberator of Malaya'

As the Japanese captured European colonies, they told the local people that they were being 'liberated' from the oppressive rule of Westerners. Japan was winning back 'Asia for the Asians'. But their treatment of people in such places as Malaya shows that the Japanese had little respect for the Asians and their rule was sometimes brutal.

The Japanese were determined to run Malaya for their benefit, and to make the local people obey them. They introduced a series of measures designed to prevent opposition to their rule.

- Anyone caught resisting the rule of the Japanese was dealt with very harshly. There were numerous arrests, and torture and public execution were common.

- The head of each family was made responsible for the family's behaviour. If anyone in the family misbehaved, the head of the family was punished.

- To encourage the locals to appreciate the Japanese culture, all schools had to teach their pupils to speak Japanese. The singing of the Japanese national anthem was also made compulsory.

### Hideki Tojo (1884–1948)

Tojo led Japan during the Second World War. He was highly patriotic and believed that Japan's economic problems could be solved by winning land and raw materials abroad. He commanded the Japanese forces against the Chinese in the 1930s and was later appointed Minister of War. In 1941, as Prime Minister, he launched the attack on Pearl Harbor. In 1945 he was arrested as a war criminal and tried to commit suicide. He failed, was found guilty and hanged in 1948.

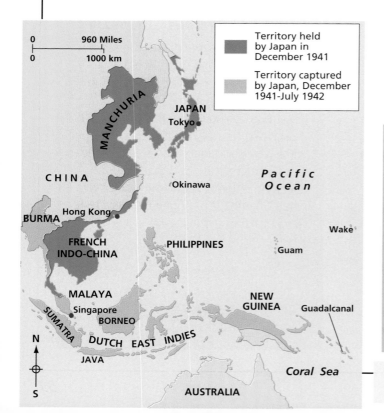

The Japanese conquest of South-East Asia in 1941–2.

Japanese soldiers executing Malayan citizens.

## The effects of occupation

The Japanese occupation of Malaya had a devastating effect on the people of Malaya. Not only were they forced to accept a harsh foreign rule, but they also saw a dramatic fall in their standard of living.

The Japanese captured Malaya from the British. As British troops retreated, they smashed everything they thought might be of value to the Japanese. Railways, bridges and roads were destroyed and vital equipment in the profitable tin and rubber industries was put out of action. This led to widespread poverty and unemployment in Malaya.

There was also a dramatic decrease in the standard of health care in Malaya. The Japanese took most of the available medicines for their army, so there was little left for the local people. Diseases such as dysentery and malaria caused many deaths. People were more susceptible to disease because they were undernourished as a result of food shortages.

It is no surprise that the people of Malaya were very pleased to see their Japanese conquerors defeated in 1945.

## Japan on the retreat

Japan's attack on Pearl Harbor had been a gamble. The Japanese hoped that by the time the American fleet was rebuilt their position would be so strong that the USA would not want to go to war with them. They were wrong. By the middle of 1942 the Americans had rebuilt their fleet and won several decisive naval battles. American forces began recapturing Japanese gains one by one. As each island was captured, the Americans built an airfield ready to support the next attack. They called their policy 'island hopping'.

The Americans often suffered heavy casualties, but Japanese losses were greater. For example, the Japanese were so determined to defend the Philippines that by the time the Americans recaptured it, 170,000 Japanese soldiers had been killed.

By mid-1945 the Japanese had been pushed back to their homeland and American bombers were pounding Japanese cities. Their position was hopeless, but they would not surrender. US army chiefs were worried. If they invaded Japan, it was bound to cost hundreds of thousands of American soldiers' lives. What were they to do?

## Little Boy and Fat Man – unwelcome visitors

The Americans did not suffer heavy casualties invading Japan, because that invasion never took place. Instead President Truman decided to use a deadly new weapon which the Allies had been developing. For some years scientists in America had been working on the 'Manhattan Project'. They were trying to use recent scientific discoveries to produce an 'atomic bomb' which would be capable of destroying small cities. By late 1945 they were ready.

At 8.15 a.m. Colonel Paul Tibbets and his crew flew the B-29 bomber, the *Enola Gay*, above Hiroshima. They were carrying an atomic bomb, nick-named 'Little Boy'. As the bomb exploded, Tibbets cried 'My God, what have we done?' Below most of the city was destroyed and 80,000 people were killed. That number increased to 140,000 by the end of the year.

Terrifying though the consequences were, the Japanese government did not surrender. It was hoping to persuade the Soviet Union to negotiate peace terms with the Americans. So three days later the Americans dropped 'Fat Man' on Nagasaki and another 70,000 Japanese men, women and children were killed. The Japanese now surrendered, but had the USA been justified in what it had done?

## Source B

Part of the order issued to drop the atomic bomb in August 1945.

### TOP SECRET

To:
General Carl Spaatz
Commanding General
United States Army Strategic Air Forces

**1** The 20th air force will deliver its first special bomb as soon as weather will permit visual bombing after about 3 August 1945. The target will be one of Hiroshima, Kokura, Niigata or Nagasaki. Additional aircraft will accompany the plane, carrying civilian scientific personnel to observe and record the effects of the bomb. The observing planes will stay several miles distant from the point of impact of the bomb.

**2** Additional bombs will be delivered on the above targets as soon as they are made ready by project staff.

## Damage caused by the bomb at Nagasaki

Area of damage:
  6.7 square kilometres
Houses completely destroyed
  or burned: 12,900
Houses badly damaged: 5509
Number killed: 73,884
Number injured: 74,909

## Source C

Henry Stimpson, who, as American Secretary of War, agreed to the dropping of the atomic bomb, explaining in 1947 why he believed it was the correct decision.

**The Allies would have been faced with the enormous task of destroying an armed force of five million men and five thousand suicide aircraft. We estimated that if we were forced to invade, the major fighting would not end until the end of 1946 at the earliest and might be expected to cost over a million casualties to American forces alone.**

## Source D

A criticism made by the US Admiral Leahy in 1950. Leahy had been adviser to President Truman in 1945.

**In my opinion the use of this barbarous weapon at Hiroshima and Nagasaki was of no material assistance in our war against Japan. The Japanese were already defeated and were ready to surrender because of the effective sea blockade and the successful bombing with conventional weapons.**

# Source E

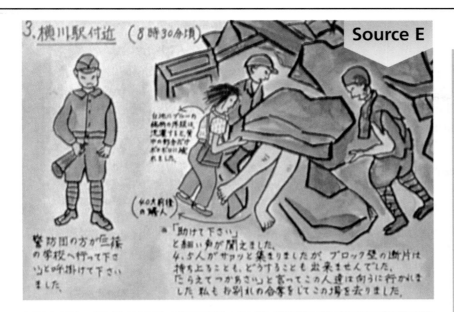

This picture was one of a number painted in 1975 by a survivor of the bomb, who is describing a scene she witnessed. The Japanese words tell of how a woman has asked for help, but people are unable to lift the concrete block off her. *Saying 'Forgive us' the others left her as she was. I prayed for her and then left also.*

## Source F

A description of the fears of a young girl badly injured in the Hiroshima explosion.

**Every so often someone searching amongst the wounded would pass by, and though it was agonising, she would raise her body slightly, whisper her name and address and beg them to contact her parents. Once she heard someone say, 'That poor girl is going to die' and from then on she determined to stay awake, afraid that if she let herself doze off, it would be her last sleep.**

## Source G

A Hiroshima father describing the death of his daughter.

**My daughter had no burns and only minor external wounds, but on 4 September she suddenly became very sick. She had spots all over her body. Her hair began to fall out. She vomited small clumps of blood many times. After ten days of agony she died.**

### Harry S. Truman (1884–1972)

Truman was President of the United States 1945 –1953 and is famous as the man who ordered the atomic bombing of Hiroshima and Nagasaki.

He fought in the First World War and first entered politics as a Democrat in 1922. He rose through the ranks and in 1944 he became vice-President when Roosevelt was elected to his fourth term of office.

When Roosevelt died in April 1945 Truman became President. He carried out a policy of opposing communism around the world. In 1949 he helped set up Nato, a military alliance providing common defence against the 'communist threat'.

He was re-elected in 1948, but decided not to stand in 1952 and retired to his home town in Kansas.

## Source H

The scene at Hiroshima after the blast.

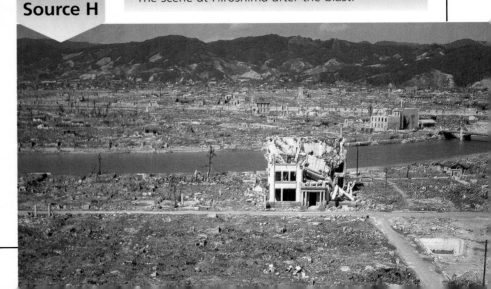

## What was the Holocaust?

The Holocaust was the Nazi answer to the fact that the ever-expanding Nazi state was full of 'undesirable' people. These people had to be destroyed. 'Holocaust' means 'wholesale destruction'.

## Who were the undesirables?

Most undesirable were people who were not 'Aryan' – Aryans had 'purely' German blood. The most undesirable people of all to Nazis were the Jews. Even before the Nazis got into power, they made their anti-Jewish feelings clear. Once in power they began to make life hard for Jews, encouraging them to leave Germany. Laws, like the 1935 Nuremberg Laws, stopped Jews from working in professions such as teaching and law. They also made rules against Jews owning dogs and using public parks or swimming pools.

While Jews were the main targets, there were other undesirables too. Black people, the physically and mentally handicapped, homosexuals, gypsies and otherwise acceptable Germans who spoke out against the Nazis were all undesirable too.

## What happened to them?

Many mentally and physically handicapped people were shut up in asylums, where some of them were experimented on and killed. Many black people were sterilised (operated on so they could not have children). Gypsies, homosexuals, black people, non-Aryans and political opponents were shut up in concentration camps. Jews who remained in Germany were put into concentration camps or herded into city ghettos – walled-off areas of the city for Jews only (set up mostly in Polish towns). Jews from all walks of life were crammed into these ghettos.

## What was a concentration camp?

Concentration camps were places where 'undesirable' people were herded together. Other countries, including America and Britain, had used camps like this for captured enemy soldiers in wartime. Nazi concentration camps were to have a very different purpose, as we shall see.

Removing those who starved to death in the Warsaw Ghetto. The ghetto is behind the wall.

**Source A**

## Esther and Perec Zylberberg

The numbers involved in the Holocaust are huge. It is easy to lose sight of real people. So we will follow two people through it – Esther and Perec Zylberberg. They lived in Lodz, Poland. The Nazis set up the first ghetto in Lodz in May, 1940. Perec was 16, Esther was 12.

## Lodz Ghetto

The ghetto was in the most run-down part of the city. It was mostly one-room flats. There were 31,720 of these flats. Only 700 had running water. About 200,000 Jews were crammed into the ghetto. The Nazis sent thousands more Jews there, from all over the lands occupied by the Nazis. They began to move people out, too. No one knew where these people were going. They were told they were being resettled, on farmland, outside the Nazi state. They had to pay for tickets and were told to take their valuables with them.

**Source B**

## ESTHER AND PEREC ZYLBERBERG

The Germans attacked Poland on 1 September, 1939. They bombed several places at once, including Lodz. The army reached the city on 8 September.

**Perec**: *We went to visit relatives who lived near the city centre. As we came to the city centre the first motorbike came into view. The thing that struck me was the clapping when they arrived. It was all those Germans who had been living in Poland, as Poles. So they had a ready-made occupation machine. My mother said Germans were hard, but fair. A lot of people of her generation thought like that.*

**Esther**: *We were terrorised from the very beginning, before the ghetto was set up. I was very scared, but I also had a kind of childish excitement that 'It's going to be over soon and my, won't there be a lot to talk about!' The French and British were in the war now. The French had the best army and the British ruled the seas. The first painful thing for us as a family was that my father had to flee, because he was an active member of the **Bund**. My brother David went too, to the Russian army. I never saw them again.*

### The Chronicle

The people of Lodz kept day-by-day secret records which survived the war. They tell us about conditions in the ghetto at the time. They also tell us of the hopes people had that the Nazis would soon be beaten, or that they would accept the Jews as useful and treat them better so they could work harder. They did not know what was about to happen.

### Lodz: sealed off from the world

Lodz was rapidly Germanised. It was renamed Litzmannstadt. 83,000 Germans, all approved by the Nazis, were moved into the city and settled in the houses in districts around the ghetto. No Jews were allowed to work outside the ghetto. In this way Lodz was sealed off tighter than any other ghetto in Nazi held areas. There was no way for friends on the outside to contact people inside to give them news, food or anything else.

## The Final Solution

Many Jews died in the ghettos, of sickness or starvation, but they were not dying quickly enough for many Nazis. As the army advanced on Russia, special killing squads were sent to kill Jews in newly-captured areas. But this was 'a waste of bullets' and still too slow. So in 1941 the Nazis used camps to kill Jews – their Final Solution to the problem. Camps were set up in isolated places which could be reached by railway. There were three sorts:

- **concentration camps:** prison camps. Here, prisoners mostly died from sickness, starvation and overwork.
- **labour camps:** larger camps where prisoners were used as slave labour in factories built nearby. Conditions were harsher, but, again, people mainly died from starvation, sickness and overwork.
- **death camps:** camps for killing people as quickly and economically as possible.

Camps were sometimes combined for efficiency. So Auschwitz had a concentration camp (Auschwitz I), a death camp (Auschwitz II/Birkenau) and a labour camp with factories (Auschwitz III).

## Source C

From the *Chronicle* of the Lodz ghetto. Jews taken from the ghetto were told they would be 'resettled' outside the Nazi state. But they suspected something more sinister was going on.

**Saturday, 15 July 1944: Today the Council Elder was told to halt resettlement. People hugged in the streets; kissed in the workshops. 'Resettlement's over!' No one thought whether this was only a brief interruption or a final halt to the transports. One thing is certain: no transport is being prepared for Monday. The ghetto has lost the habit of thinking more than a few hours ahead.**

## The industry of death

One of the most gruesome things about the death camps was how the Nazis kept 'improving' them. The first people taken from the Lodz ghetto (from January 1942 onwards) were taken to Chelmno death camp. In four months 54,979 Jews left Lodz to die at Chelmno. They were loaded into sealed vans and gassed with exhaust fumes. But this was still not efficient enough. And it used up petrol. In July 1944 the transports from Lodz stopped. Chelmno had been shut down. A new and more efficient system had been set up: gas chambers. The next transports from Lodz went to Auschwitz and its death camp, Birkenau. The Nazis now re-used every part of the people they murdered – their clothing, their hair, their teeth, their ashes. They tried to re-use their fat, too. But people who are starving to death have none.

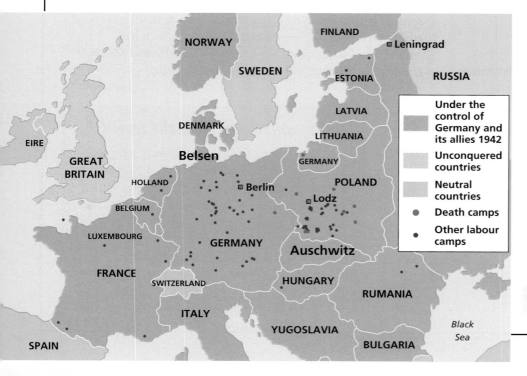

The Nazi camps.

## Source D

The platform at Auschwitz where people were divided up into groups. Some went to the labour camp. Others went straight to the death camp, Auschwitz/Birkenau. This is what happened to Esther's mother, Sara Zylberberg.

**Perec:** *The deportations got more frequent. There were already fears about what they meant. Work was a passport to staying on. I managed to get my mother and my sister into the carpet-making plant. We were undernourished, disease-ridden, in constant fear of almost everything.*
Perec was 19 when he was transported to a labour camp at Czestochowa.
*The work was hard. There weren't many machines, we did most of the hauling of machine parts. The German guards carried whips and there were regular whippings, but we were not beaten too often. It was a business-like slave compound. There were Germans in charge, but they set up Jewish foremen and police. On 15 January 1945 we were woken early, given some bread and coffee and told to pack our belongings.*
The Russians were close to Czestochowa. The workers marched deeper into Germany, to Buchenwald labour camp. It had all sorts of 'undesirables', even US war prisoners.
*We were almost shoeless and dressed in tattered trousers, with no underwear or coats. The frosts were terrible. We had to clear the rubble when a nearby city was bombed. It was the first time I had seen ordinary Germans. Now and again a woman would give us a potato or a piece of bread.*

**Esther:** *The most painful moments in the ghetto were the mass deportations. Most of my friends were disappearing. All the people who were deported were never heard of again. Clothing started to arrive back, marked with names. People found their relatives' clothes.*
Esther and her mother were deported together, to Auschwitz.
*We had been under Nazi occupation for so long, and suffered degradation, hunger and disease, but we were not prepared for what Auschwitz was. We thought we were being sent to another place of work. When we arrived we said 'where are we?' The railway people said 'You mean you don't know what this place is?' I had seen the barbed wire, people looking mad. We did not think we would stop there. It looked like a lunatic asylum. They gave us a tin of food on arrival, to eat while we were being pushed towards selection. This was the most painful moment, which I have never got over – separation from my mother.*

### Allies in Auschwitz

There were 1200 British prisoners of war at Auschwitz. They were kept in Auschwitz III and worked on extending the factory area. They saw Jewish labour camp workers being beaten and otherwise maltreated. But the whole Auschwitz site was so huge that they only heard rumours about what went on at Auschwitz II/Birkenau.

## Liberation and after

As the Russians advanced on Germany, camps in Poland (including Auschwitz) were closed down. People were marched to camps closer to the centre of Germany. Many died on the way. Allied soldiers who reached the camps found only those few who had hidden or had been left to die. They found piles of dead bodies, huge mounds marking mass graves and vast heaps of ashes with fragments of bones. They began to realise the scale of the killing.

## What happened to the survivors?

The Nazis nearly wiped out all Jews in Nazi-occupied areas. But there were survivors. They were cared for in hospitals until they could be moved. Then they had to cope with the rest of their lives. Most had lost many relatives. They had lost their homes, their possessions, their health. Many of the children were taken to other countries and found homes and work. But they had a great deal to adjust to. Most people were kind, but could not understand what the children had lived through. The emphasis was on getting them working, not replacing the years of schooling they had lost.

## Source F

The British journalist Patrick Gordon Walker wrote this account of Belsen, a labour camp, not a death camp. (Esther Zylberberg was marched here from Auschwitz.)

Corpses in every state of decay were lying around, piled on top of each other in heaps. People, walking skeletons, were falling dead all around. One woman came up to a soldier and asked for milk for her baby. The man took the baby and saw it had been dead for days, black in the face and shrivelled up. She went on begging for milk. So he poured some on the dead lips. The mother carried the baby off, stumbled and fell dead after a few yards.

Five thousand people have died here in nine days. We found an Englishman, half dead. He had a bullet in his back. He had been shot by a guard while crawling about days before. Everywhere there was the smell of death. Many people have typhus and dysentery. Most of the girls here are Jews from Auschwitz. Over and over I hear the same story of the parades where people were picked out for the gas chambers. To you at home, this is one camp. There are many more. This is what you are fighting. None of this is propaganda. It is the simple truth.

**Source E**

Just one of the hundreds of mass graves found by Allies in Nazi concentration camps.

## Source G

Some of Esther's and Perec's family, before Esther was born. Perec (the baby on the right) is the only one from this photo who survived the Holocaust.

Esther and Perec made it through the Holocaust. They nearly didn't. Both were moved on ahead of the advancing Allied armies. Both were ill when their camps were liberated. The sick were dumped in 'hospitals' to die.

Perec was moved by train.

**Perec:** *We passed through bombed-out cities. At Chemnitz we could see from the open trucks right across the bombed buildings to the other side of the city. It warmed our hearts. There is a sort of fog surrounding that journey in my memory. I seem to remember eating grass, leaves, bark. The trains went backwards and forwards and we lost count of the days and nights. Eventually we must have got somewhere. I remember people yelling, commands. We disembarked. I heard about half the transport died, that some dead were eaten. I don't remember seeing that, but that's what I heard. Then I wasn't in a freight car. I was in a building with bunks. I don't know who was in charge, Red Cross or Germans. There were quite a few nurses, I remember that. I remember being in a bed, clinging to a piece of bread. I kept grabbing for it and people calmed me down, showed it to me. A nurse told me that I had typhus and was in a clinic. The next thing I remember is a tank outside the window and thinking: the Allies are here.*

Perec was one of 732 young people taken to England. They went to hostels in the Lake District and then to homes all over the country. Perec tried to track down his family. Only Esther could be found. Perec moved to Canada in 1958 and set up in the clothing business. He still lives there.

**Esther:** *When I came to, everyone was going mad. There was murder in everyone's hearts, probably in mine too. Despite the fact that I knew what had happened to my mother, I had to keep on believing that somehow it wasn't true. I prayed with all my might, I don't know who to, probably myself, 'please let me not be damaged for the whole of my life. Let me keep some love for people.'*

Esther was taken to Sweden. In April 1947 she came to England.

*I lived with an elderly Jewish couple. They treated me well, but could not really understand me. I longed to continue my education, to train as a nurse, but no one was prepared to give me my keep while I tried to replace my lost years.*

Esther married another Holocaust survivor, Stasiek Brunstein. They had two children. Esther now lives in London.

### You must forget

Perec Zylberberg says of the adults who looked after the children who arrived in England: *Very little was ever said about the atrocities of the war, about our personal experiences.* They were expected to forget, to put the past behind them. It was almost like denying it had happened.

Britain and the USA had always been uneasy in an alliance with the USSR because of their political differences. Less than a year after winning the Second World War, they were openly talking about the USSR as an enemy. For over 40 years the two sides were so hostile to each other that historians call it 'the Cold War' – 'Cold' because they never actually went to war.

## Why were they hostile?

The main reason for hostility was their different economic and political systems. The USSR was a communist state. The USA and Britain were capitalist states. Many people, in both countries, believed communism and capitalism could not exist alongside each other for long. One system would take over the other. Both sides were determined not to be taken over.

## Buffer zones

In the USSR, Stalin wanted a **buffer zone** – friendly countries between the USSR and possible enemies in the west. The USSR had been invaded from the west before. British, French and US troops had invaded to help the anti-communists in the Civil War, in 1919 and 1920. Hitler had invaded the USSR in 1941. Stalin set up 'satellite states' between the USSR and the West. They governed themselves, but were communist and dominated by the USSR. Anyone invading the USSR from the west would have to invade these countries first.

## One goes, they all go

The USA and Britain feared communism would spread to the West through eastern Europe. Some leaders believed the 'domino theory'. They felt if one country became communist, it would set off another and another. It would be like knocking over the first in a line of upright dominoes – each domino would knock the next one over. They were desperate to stop any country becoming the first communist domino.

**Eastern European communist governments set up:** Yugoslavia (1945), Bulgaria (1947), Poland, Czechoslovakia, Hungary, Romania (1948).

**Vietnam, 1959–75:** The USA sent money, weapons and troops to South Vietnam to help the government fight communist **guerrillas** who were backed by the North Vietnamese. The US troops could not defeat the communist guerrillas, so withdrew in 1973. Two years later South Vietnam became a communist state.

**Cuba, 1962:** Cuba became a communist country in 1959, after a revolution led by Fidel Castro. The Soviets asked Castro to let them build a missile base in Cuba. This would put most of the USA in range of Soviet missiles. The USA ordered a naval blockade of Cuba to stop the missiles arriving. For a while it looked as if nuclear war would break out. At the last minute the USSR climbed down and abandoned the plans for a missile base.

**Czechoslovakia, 1968; Poland, 1981:** There was opposition to communist rule in both countries. The opposition was crushed each time with the help of Soviet troops.

**The collapse of eastern European communism, 1989:** Reforms in the USSR lessened communist power. Revolutions in satellite countries kicked out communist governments. First went Poland, then East Germany, Hungary, Czechoslovakia, Bulgaria and Romania. In December the Soviet leader, Gorbachev, and the US President, Bush, declared the Cold War over. Later that month the demolition of the Berlin Wall began.

**NATO, 1949:** The North Atlantic Treaty Organisation was an alliance between the USA, Britain, France, Canada, Portugal, Norway, Belgium, the Netherlands and Italy. They promised to defend each other against attack from the USSR.

**People's Republic of China, 1949:** The Chinese Communist Party (with help from the USSR) won the Chinese Civil War. China became a communist country, but did not have good relations with the USSR.

**The division of Germany, 1949:** At the end of the Second World War, the USSR occupied one half of Germany. Britain, France and the USA occupied the other. Eventually Germany became two countries: communist East Germany and capitalist West Germany.

**The Korean War, 1950–3:** After the Second World War the USA occupied South Korea, the USSR, North Korea. Each set up its own government. The communist North Koreans invaded the south. The USA and its allies sent troops to help South Korea. China sent troops to the north. The two sides made peace in 1953, agreeing to make two separate countries.

**The Warsaw Pact, 1955:** After West Germany was allowed to join NATO in 1955, the USSR and its allies (Romania, Poland, East Germany, Bulgaria, Czechoslovakia and Hungary) set up the Warsaw Pact – an alliance against the Western powers.

U.S.A

CANADA

North Pole
+

New York

CHINA

USSR

INDIA

PAKISTAN

EASTERN EUROPE

Paris

Vienna

Geneva

N.A.T.O. countries

Warsaw Pact countries

**The Berlin Wall, 1961:** So many people were escaping from East to West Germany in Berlin (which was itself divided between East and West Germany) that the East German government built a wall with guardposts to stop it. To most people this was the most obvious symbol of the Cold War.

**The Hungarian Rising, 1956:** Not all satellite states were happy. Many people in Hungary wanted more freedom than their communist government gave them. They rebelled. After five days of fighting, Soviet troops moved into Hungary and crushed the rising. Hungary stayed communist and in the Warsaw Pact.

## Reds Under the Bed

In 1950 the Republican Senator Joe McCarthy announced in the US Senate that the State Department and the US army were full of communists, deliberately planted there to subvert the USA. He said he had a list of 200 names of people who worked for the government who were communist sympathisers. These accusations sparked off a wave of anti-Communist hysteria which spread like wildfire. One opponent coined the phrase 'seeing Reds under the bed', which stuck.

But the effect of the hysteria was far from funny. For four years lists were drawn up of possible communist sympathisers. People were investigated by a Committee on Un-American Activities.

People had to swear they were not, nor had ever been, communist, just to keep their jobs. Starting with people in government office the McCarthy 'witch hunts' spread to all kinds of people, even film stars. Some people were driven to suicide. By the time McCarthy's claims had been discredited, many lives had been ruined.

The box on Cuba, 1962, on page 68, says: *The USA ordered a naval blockade of Cuba*. It sounds like a simple decision, easily made. But it was only made after days of almost constant discussion, consultation with US allies and negotiations with the USSR. Tapes of the discussions, made by President Kennedy, were made public in 1997. They give us an insight into the uncertainty and disagreement behind the final statement of government policy. During the crisis, no one knew what would happen. Both sides had to consider the possibility of nuclear war. Both sides wanted to avoid this. But they also wanted to avoid giving in.

## What sparked off the crisis?

On 16 October, 1962, US planes took secret photos that showed Russian missiles, capable of carrying nuclear warheads, on the island of Cuba. For the first time in history the USA would be within reach of Russian nuclear missiles. Frantic debate followed between the US President and his advisers about what to do.

## What happened?

After days of discussion, consultation with experts and US allies and negotiations with the USSR, the President and his advisers reached a decision. On 22 October they ordered a naval blockade of Cuba. After several tense days, where there was a serious possibilty of nuclear war, the USSR backed down. The next page gives part of the debate on the first day of the crisis.

The crisis had so concerned the leaders of the USSR and the USA that in 1963 they agreed to set up a direct telephone link between Moscow and Washington, now called the 'hot line'.

### Why Cuba?

How were the Russians able to send nuclear weapons to Cuba, an island that was far closer to the USA than to the USSR? The USA had once had a great deal of influence over Cuba, until 1959, when the government was overthrown by Fidel Castro. Once he was in power, Castro began to make reforms which looked suspiciously like communism to the Americans. So the new US President, John F. Kennedy, told the CIA to help some Cuban exiles try to overthrow Castro. They invaded in April 1961 and, despite all the American help, failed miserably. The invasion made Castro more anti-American and he accepted help and later weapons from the USSR.

**Source A**

LAUNCH PAD WITH ERECTOR
CHERRY PICKER
LAUNCH PAD WITH ERECTOR
MISSILE READY BLDGS.
OXIDIZER VEHICLES
FUELING VEHICLES

One of the pictures that started it all. Many of them are hard to interpret, but in this one you can see the missile carriers clearly. The labels were put on at the time by the Americans.

MRBM = Medium Range Ballistic Missile.

## *16 OCTOBER MORNING*

**Lundahl**: *There's a missile launch site and 2 new military encampments on the southern edge of Sierra del Rosario.*

**President Kennedy**: *How do you know its a missile?*

**Lundahl**: *The length, sir.*

**President Kennedy**: *Is it ready to be fired?*

**Graybeal**: *No sir.*

**President Kennedy**: *How long have we got?*

**Graybeal**: *If the equipment's checked sir, you're talking about a matter of hours.*

**Rusk**: *Do we assume these are nuclear?*

**McNamarra**: *There's no question about that. We don't know where the warheads are, how soon they can be armed. It could take hours, even days, to be ready.*

**Rusk**: *Sir, this is serious. We have to get rid of this base. Do we do an unannounced strike, or build up pressure until the other side has to act or give in? We could make a quick strike – not invade, or start a war, make it clear we were just wiping out the base. Or we can eliminate the problem by eliminating the whole island. Or we could take the political route. Make it clear we know what's going on. Demand to inspect the site. Whatever we do, we should call up troops. We need to get onto NATO. Blockade Cuba. No flights; get the British to stop trade. We face a situation that could well lead to general war.*

**McNamarra**: *If we're going to bomb these installations, it has to be before they are armed. There's no knowing when that will be. We'll have to hit the missile sites, air bases, any hidden aircraft and possible nuclear storage sites. This would be a big strike. We'd kill a lot of Cubans, 2–3000. We would have to follow up, invade.*

**President Kennedy**: *So you're talking about:*

1  *Strike just the bases.*
2  *Strike bases, airfields and anything else connected with the missile sites.*
3  *Do that **and** blockade as well.*

*There's the question of allied consultation. Don't think it'll be a lot of use. Probably ought to tell them, though, night before.*

**Robert Kennedy**: *We have to decide whether to invade. If we do the full air strike, we'll kill a lot of people. So the Russians will either send in more missiles  or strike our missiles in Turkey or Iran.*

**Rusk**: *You might as well. Do the whole job.*

**President Kennedy**: *We need to work out what we need to do in the next 24 hours to be ready for any option. Let's meet tonight, after you've consulted. As we don't know how soon the missiles can be ready, we have to start preparing to take them out. Because that's what we're going to do anyway. We're certainly going to do No 1. We're going to take out these missiles.*

## *16 OCTOBER EVENING*

**McNamarra**: *We could start with a limited air attack. But the Soviets would respond, militarily, somewhere in the world. It may be worth that price. But we must recognise that the price is there. And we should be ready to mobilise our troops to counter it.*

**President Kennedy**: *The chances of it becoming a broader struggle increase each time you step it up. If you do all those air strikes, then you might as well invade.*

**Taylor**: *I don't think we should invade.*

**McNamarra**: *Circumstances might force us to. And we might be forced to blockade.*

**Robert Kennedy**: *Then you'd have to sink Russian ships and submarines. Shouldn't we get it over with and take our losses? Hell, if he sticks those kinds of missiles in after the warning then he's gonna get a war, when he does. So...*

**McNamarra**: *Which supports the point I was making. We ought to get the options down and work out the consequences.*

**Who's who?**

This list covers those people speaking in this extract. Others were involved in the debates.

**Political advisors**: Robert Kennedy (the President's brother), Robert McNamarra (Secretary of Defense), Dean Rusk (Secretary of State).

**Military advisors**: General Maxwell Taylor, Arthur Lundahl (an expert on interpreting photographs), Sidney Graybeal (a missile expert).

Have you ever wondered why so many people in the world speak English, French or Spanish? The answer lies in the fact that until recently each of the major European countries had an overseas empire. Most of the Spanish Empire had gained independence by 1900, but when the Second World War broke out in 1939, Britain and France still had vast empires, covering over a quarter of the world. Within the next 30 years those empires vanished. Why?

## The effects of the Second World War (1939–45)

In 1940 Germans troops occupied much of western Europe and threatened to invade Britain. People living in the colonies of the defeated nations watched these developments with interest. They had always thought their European masters were mighty nations that could not be challenged. Now they saw that this was not the case. This led many of them to lose respect for Europeans and consider how best to win back their independence.

For some countries the answer was already at hand. The Japanese realised that the European countries were fighting for their own survival and could not protect their colonies. So in South-East Asia, Japan invaded and occupied European colonies. At first the Japanese were welcomed as liberators, but their brutal treatment of the local inhabitants soon changed this. When Japan was defeated and the Europeans returned, they found that their colonies were no longer prepared to be ruled by foreigners. Independence was soon to follow, though sometimes only after fierce fighting.

**Source A**

Mahatma Gandhi. He was so respected in India that even when he was imprisoned by the British in 1928 for encouraging opposition to their rule, the judge described him as *in a different category from any person I have ever tried, or am likely to try.*

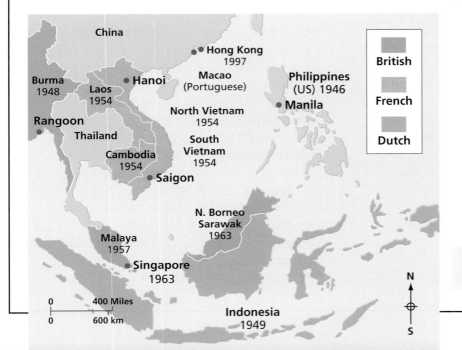

How South-East Asia became independent.

## Economic problems

Britain and France won the war, but at a great economic cost. In 1945 Britain was in debt to the USA and found it hard to pay to run an empire. The new Labour government, elected in 1945, wanted to make India independent, but was worried about violence between Muslims and Hindus. In the end the subcontinent was divided into India (mainly Hindu) and Pakistan (mainly Muslim). Ceylon (now Sri Lanka) also became independent.

## The growth of nationalism

One of the benefits of European rule was that it brought widespread education to local people. But education introduced the idea that people should govern themselves. This led **nationalist** leaders (such as Gandhi in India, and Jomo Kenyatta in Kenya) to ask why this did not apply to their own countries. They carried out campaigns for independence and used mistakes made by Europeans, such as the Amritsar Massacre (see pages 74–5), to win support for their cause.

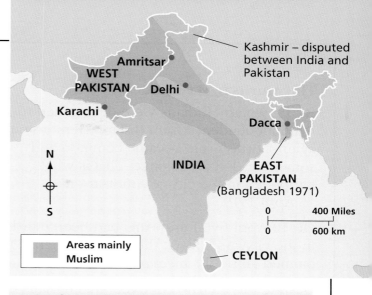

India after independence.

In Africa, in particular, freedom fighters began to carry out wars against their European masters, and independence, in places such as Algeria and Indonesia, was won only after fierce fighting.

By 1970 the European empires were gone. Some small remnants of empire remained – mostly places such as St Helena and Montserrat, financed by European countries – and not wanting independence.

How Africa became independent.

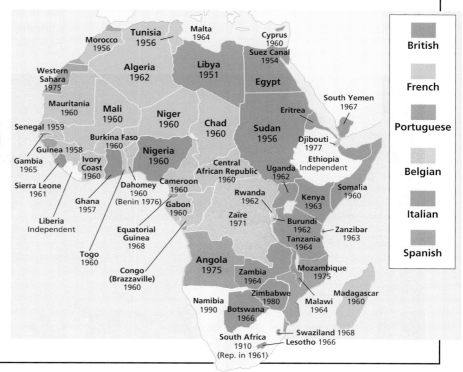

### Gandhi (1869–1948)

Gandhi was an Indian Hindu who trained in England as a lawyer. In 1893 he moved to South Africa where the ill-treatment of Indians helped him develop his method of non-violent opposition to injustice. On his return to India in 1915 he used this method to oppose British rule and was imprisoned on several occasions. He was widely respected by people of all religions and his threat to fast to the death helped quell fighting between Hindus and Muslims in 1946–7. He was assassinated by a Hindu extremist in 1948.

## The Amritsar Massacre

By 1919 many Indians were determined to win independence from Britain. Demonstrations against British rule became common and sometimes led to violence. This is what happened in the city of Amritsar on 13 April 1919.

On 10 April five Europeans had been murdered in the city. As a result the British General Dyer banned all public meetings in the area.

Despite this a crowd of over 5000 Indians met in an area known as the Jallianwala Bagh to hear speeches criticising the British. Although the meeting was peaceful and contained large numbers of men, women and children, General Dyer was determined to break it up. He took his troops to the Jallianwala Bagh and positioned them on high ground near the narrow entrance. He ordered his troops to open fire on the crowd without warning.

The Jallianwala Bagh was surrounded by a wall five feet high and there were few exits. Official British figures state that nearly two thousand men, women and children were wounded or killed. The British set up the Hunter Committee to investigate the incident and General Dyer was dismissed from his command.

## Source C

An extract from *The Times*, 27 May 1920.

**General Dyer, with a very small force, opened fire upon a dense crowd assembled in a confined space. His soldiers fired 1650 times, killing 379 persons and possibly wounding three times as many. The government has since stated that although there were problems in the area, Dyer was not entitled to select for punishment an unarmed crowd which had committed no acts of violence, had made no attempts to oppose him by force, and many of whom must have been unaware that they were breaking his order.**

## Source D

An extract from the *Daily Mail*, 4 May 1920.

**TINY LOYAL FORCE AGAINST GREAT CROWD OF INDIANS**

**General Dyer issued orders against violence and damage to property, and against meetings of more than four people. Despite this, the Indians gathered in large numbers at Jallianwala Bagh – estimates vary between 5000 and 30,000. It was then that Dyer, who was in command of a little force of less than a hundred soldiers and two armoured cars, gave the order to fire.**

**Source B**

A scene from the film *Gandhi* showing Dyer's troops firing on the crowd.

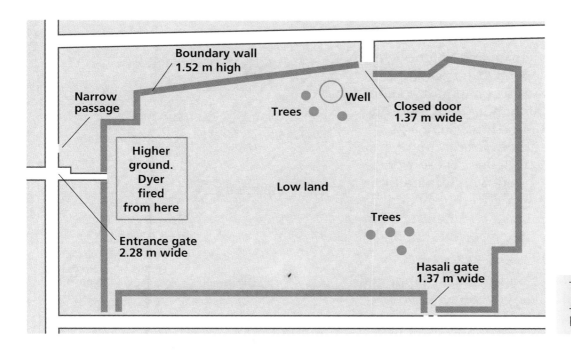

The Jallianwala Bagh.

Labels on the map:
- Boundary wall 1.52 m high
- Narrow passage
- Trees
- Well
- Closed door 1.37 m wide
- Higher ground. Dyer fired from here
- Low land
- Trees
- Entrance gate 2.28 m wide
- Hasali gate 1.37 m wide

## Source E

Part of an interview with General Dyer in the *Daily Mail* on 4 May 1920.

**I had to shoot. I had thirty seconds to make up my mind about what action to take. What would have happened if I had not shot? I and my little force would have been swept away and then what would have happened?**

## Source F

Part of the evidence given by General Dyer to the Hunter Committee.

*Question:* You did not issue a warning to the crowd to disperse before you opened fire. Did you think you were going to be attacked?

*Dyer:* The situation in the area was very serious. It was no longer a question of merely dispersing the crowd. I had to produce a sufficient impression of strength not only on those who were there, but throughout that part of India.

*Question:* When did you decide to fire?

*Dyer:* When I first heard of the meeting.

*Question:* If the entrance into the Jallianwala Bagh had been wide enough to allow your armoured cars in, would you have used their machine guns on the crowd?

*Dyer:* I think, probably, yes.

### General Dyer (1862–1927)

Reginald Edward Harry Dyer was forced to resign from the army in 1920 following his actions at Amritsar. He was, however, a very experienced and able soldier who had shown great leadership skills during his period of service in India and had risen to the rank of brigadier-general.

Dyer was born in India and was educated at the Royal Military College at Sandhurst in England. He transferred to the Indian Army and took part in military campaigns in 1886–1908 and again in 1916 - with great success. He was responsible for maintaining order in India following disturbances in 1919 before his controversial action at Amritsar.

# 3.4 THE WAR IN VIETNAM

## Why was there a war?

In 1954 North Vietnam and South Vietnam gained their independence from France. North Vietnam was a communist country led by Ho Chi Minh, but South Vietnam was anti-communist. However, inside South Vietnam there was a group of armed rebels called the Vietcong. These were communist supporters who wanted to overthrow their own government and make South Vietnam a communist country. Not surprisingly they received support from North Vietnam.

Many people in South Vietnam supported the Vietcong. Their government, led by President Ngo Dingh Diem, was corrupt and had little interest in improving the lives of its people. But the Americans were keen supporters of Diem. He was strongly anti-communist, and so in their eyes was an ideal person to govern South Vietnam.

## The domino theory

One of the reasons why the United States was so keen to prevent South Vietnam becoming a communist country was that it feared that once South Vietnam fell to communism, other countries would soon follow. This is called the domino theory, because it is like a collection of upright dominoes falling one after the other.

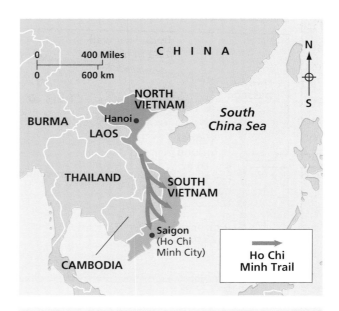

South East Asia during the Vietnam War.

As you read on pages 68–9 the Americans had been trying to prevent the spread of communism in Europe. Now it looked as if Asia, too, was under threat and the Americans were determined to defend it against communism.

In 1955 the United States began sending 'military advisers', weapons and supplies into Vietnam to help President Diem. Despite the assassination of Diem in 1963, the new American President, Lyndon Johnson, decided to step up American help for the new South Vietnamese government.

The domino theory.

## The war hots up

By the late 1960s the Americans had over half a million troops in Vietnam fighting the Vietcong and North Vietnam, which was giving the Vietcong supplies. The Americans had the latest equipment such as rocket launchers and helicopter gunships, but the Vietcong did not fight open battles, where these weapons could be used. Instead they fought a guerrilla war – carrying out acts of sabotage on American bases, ambushing soldiers on patrol and setting up booby traps. Then they melted back into the jungle where the Americans could not find them.

These methods made the American soldiers very frustrated, as they were usually unable to identify who had carried out the attacks. Sometimes they took their revenge on suspected Vietcong hideouts but ended up killing innocent men, women and children.

To stop North Vietnam supplying the Vietcong down a jungle pathway called the Ho Chi Minh Trail, the Americans carried out a huge bombing campaign on North Vietnam's capital, Hanoi. American planes also dropped napalm to burn back the jungle and chemicals to take the leaves off the trees. These chemicals also killed animals and people. Whole villages were moved behind barbed wire to prevent contact with the Vietcong, but support for the communists did not decline.

## Time to get out

By 1968 the United States was spending $30,000 million dollars a year and 300 of its soldiers were dying each week. At home there were huge demonstrations against the war, fuelled by news of atrocities carried out by American soldiers and pictures on television of the Vietcong attacking the American Embassy in the South Vietnamese capital, Saigon. President Nixon decided to withdraw American troops. In 1973 he managed to arrange a cease-fire between North and South Vietnam and brought the American soldiers home. Two years later North Vietnam invaded South Vietnam and united the two countries under the communist flag.

### Source A

American soldiers on patrol encounter bamboo spikes laid by the Vietcong, as described in Source B.

### Source B

A member of the Vietcong describes the best way to fight the Americans.

**Let me tell you how we fought the Americans. We knew that we did not have the weapons to fight them in the open, so we had to fight another way. For instance, we would put many pieces of sharp bamboo in the ground near the paths the Americans walked on. Then we would shoot at the Americans when they were on the paths. They jumped off the paths and onto the bamboo and got very hurt.**

**Then the Americans always did the same thing. They would be very angry and might kill some people, or shoot up some houses or have a big military operation in the area. They never found us, but made many enemies when they did these things. That was the way to fight the Americans.**

## The My Lai Massacre

On 16 March 1968 a group of 150 soldiers and five officers from the American army were landed by helicopter near the South Vietnamese village of My Lai. The soldiers had been given instructions to ensure that the village contained no members of the Vietcong. The soldiers were surprised to find that their landing did not attract Vietcong fire and that there appeared to be no sign of Vietcong in the area.

The senior officer, Lieutenant William Calley, led his troops into the village and ordered that all the inhabitants were to be rounded up. As the soldiers searched the village, some of the women were raped and other civilians were gunned down. A group of old men, women and children were herded together and shot dead.

By the time the Americans left the village, an estimated 150 unarmed civilians had been killed.

## What they said about the Massacre

### Source C

An account of the attack from a villager who survived.

Nothing was happening here. It was a very quiet life. Then the helicopters came and all the troops surrounded us. They were firing their guns and the people were dying. Oh it was horrible! I pushed my son into the paddy field and lay on top of him. Corpses fell on top of us. I told him. 'Don't cry and see if we can survive.' I lifted my head and saw Americans pointing in all directions. The people who were still alive were shot again and again. I hate the Americans. I shall never forgive them.

A photograph shows some of the dead at My Lai.

### Source D

## Source E

An army sergeant comments on the purpose of the attack.

The understanding, or the order that was given, was to kill everyone in that village. Someone asked if that meant everyone. Those people, the women, the kids, the old men, were Vietcong or they were sympathetic to the Vietcong. It was quite clear that no one was to be spared in that village.

## Source H

An American soldier comments on the problems faced by the US army in Vietnam.

You know you had little kids in Vietnam who would shoot you in the back as you walked away. I couldn't work out which people were the enemy. All of them looked the same, North Vietnamese and South Vietnamese. How could I tell?

## Source F

Comments made by Lieutenant William Calley at his trial. Calley was the only person to be convicted for the massacre at My Lai. He was given a life sentence for murder, but released after three days on the instructions of President Nixon.

My troops were being massacred in Vietnam by an enemy they could not see. The enemy was communism. When I came face to face with it, I had to put the lives of my own troops first.

## Source G

Survivors of My Lai being comforted after the massacre.

## Richard Nixon (1913–94)

Nixon is famous as the only American President to have resigned from office. Born in California, he graduated from law school in 1937. He began practising law in California before joining the United States navy in the Second World War.

In 1946 he was elected to Congress as a Republican and in 1950 was elected to the Senate, though many disapproved of the way that he used an alleged Communist scare to win support. In 1952 he became Vice President when Dwight Eisenhower was elected President.

Nixon was elected president in 1968. Then in 1972 news emerged that Watergate, the headquarters of Nixon's opponents, the Democrats had been bugged. Tapes of conversations held in the White House proved that Nixon had been involved and that he had tried to cover up what he had done. He resigned and was replaced by Gerald Ford in August 1974.

# 3.5  THE UNITED NATIONS: AN ORGANISATION FOR PEACE?

The Second World War horrified people by its terrible loss of life and destruction. The League of Nations, an organisation set up at the end of the First World War, had failed to stop a second slide into devastating conflict. In 1945, shortly after the end of the Second World War, representatives from 50 countries met in San Francisco. They were setting up an organisation which, they were determined, would this time keep world peace and enable people to live their lives to the full.

## Source A

This is the way in which the United Nations was organised.

### United Nations Secretary General

Runs the UN aided by officials from all the member states.

### Security Council

- Takes day-to-day action on behalf of the General Assembly.
- 15 members – the five great powers (UK, USA, CIS, France, China) and ten other nations elected for two years at a time.
- All decisions have to be carried by nine members voting YES and none of the Great Powers voting NO (the veto).

### General Assembly

The parliament of the United Nations.
- Each member state has one vote.
- Meets once a year in September.
- Special meetings can be held in an emergency.
- Important matters decided by a two-thirds majority; other decisions by a simple majority.

### UN ORGANIZATIONS AND AGENCIES

Other organizations and agencies do much of the most valuable work of the UN, such as WHO (health) and UNESCO (education).

## Source B

The United Nations' Charter.

**WE, THE PEOPLES OF THE UNITED NATIONS, ARE DETERMINED**

- to save succeeding generations from the scourge of war which twice in our lifetime has brought untold sorrow to mankind,
- to reaffirm faith in fundamental human rights, in the dignity and worth of the human person, in the equal rights of men and women and of nations large and small,
- to establish respect for treaties and international law,
- to promote social progress and better standards of life in larger freedom,

**AND FOR THESE ENDS**
- to practise tolerance and live together in peace with one another,
- to unite our strength to maintain international peace and security,
- to ensure that armed force shall not be used save in the common interest,
- to help the economic and social advancement of all peoples.

A cartoon published in 1945.

## Source C

RULE: All ... to play together; but not so as to cramp any player's style. (That would be unrealistic)

"A FINE TEAM – BUT COULD DO WITH A DASH OF UNITY..."

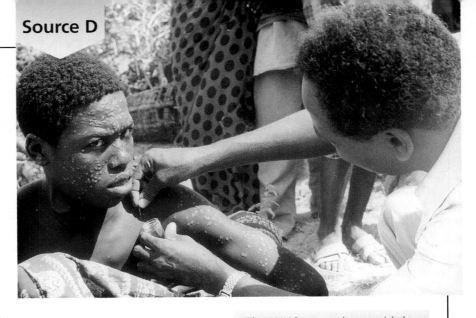

The United Nations set up various agencies which it hoped would help people in need and so bring about a better world for everyone.

- The International Court of Justice meets at The Hague in the Netherlands. Fifteen judges from different countries hear cases to do with international disputes, such as frontiers.
- The United Nations International Children's Emergency Fund looks after needy children everywhere.
- The World Health Organisation fights disease and promotes good health. In 1967 the WHO launched a campaign to wipe smallpox off the face of the earth. In 1977 a man from Somalia was the last known person to die from the disease, and two years later the whole world was smallpox free.
- The United Nations Educational, Social and Cultural Organisation promotes all aspects of learning and understanding.

The WHO campaign to rid the world of smallpox, 1967.

## UNICEF

The United Nations Children's Fund is an agency of the United Nations, concerned with the welfare of children everywhere. It was set up in 1946, immediately after the war, to help children in Europe and China. Nowadays, UNICEF sets up programmes for long-term benefits to children, especially those in developing countries who are in greatest need.

More than 139 countries receive UNICEF support for health care, nutrition, basic education and water and sanitation programmes. UNICEF works with the governments of different countries, their community leaders, teachers, parents and children.

In 1965, UNICEF was awarded the Nobel Peace prize.

**Source E**

Learning to read in Morocco, 1960. Part of UNESCO's work.

# 3.6 THE UNITED NATIONS: AN ORGANISATION FOR WAR?

One of the aims of the United Nations was to keep peace between the nations of the world. Keeping the peace, however, often meant going to war!

## Korea (1950–3)

UN troops (mainly from the USA) were sent to help South Korea when it was invaded by communist armies from North Korea.

## Suez (1956)

British, French and Israeli forces invaded the area around the Suez canal. The United Nations demanded their withdrawal and sent troops to keep the peace.

## Arab-Israeli conflict

For ten years (1957–67) UN forces patrolled the frontier between Israel and Egypt. When they left, the Arab-Israeli war broke out.

## The Congo (1960)

When the Congo became independent in 1960, law and order quickly broke down. The UN sent an army of 20,000 troops, from Canada, India, Ireland, Ghana and Nigeria, to restore peace. It also sent experts to help the country become truly self-governing and teams of doctors and food experts to help the people.

## Did the UN always intervene when peace was threatened?

The UN did not intervene directly in world crises like the rebellion in Hungary (1956), the Cuban missile crisis (1962), the Vietnam War (1959–75) or the Falklands War (1982). This was either because the Security Council and General Assembly could not agree about what should be done, or because the Great Powers simply ignored them.

**Source A**

HISTORY DOESN'T REPEAT ITSELF

The cartoonist is saying that the only way the UN can avoid the same failure as the League of Nations is by taking military action (as in Korea). Unlike the League, the UN could use force. It had no army of its own, but members loaned troops when necessary.

**Source B**

Written in 1957 by the historian David Thomson.

The power of the veto was highly valued by members of the Security Council. However, the veto made the Security Council ineffective when it came to taking action against the two superpowers, the USA and the USSR.

Part of Operation 'Desert Storm'. Katherine Jenerette is on the right.

**Source C**

## Operation Desert Storm

On 2 August 1990, Iraq invaded the tiny, oil-rich state of Kuwait in the Persian Gulf. What happened then?

- *2 August* The UN Security Council condemned the action and demanded the withdrawal of Iraqi forces.
- *9 August* The UN Security Council imposed economic and **military sanctions** on Iraq.
- *25 August* The UN Security Council called for the use of force, if necessary, to make Iraq withdraw from Kuwait.
- *29 November* The UN Security Council set a deadline of 15 January 1991 for withdrawal of Iraqi troops.
- *15 January* The deadline expired and Iraqi troops remained in Kuwait.
- *17 January* 200,000 Allied forces began 'Operation Desert Storm' with a massive air offensive to liberate Kuwait.
- *26 February* Kuwait was liberated.
- *2 March* The UN called on Iraq to revoke all claims on Kuwait.
- *5 April* The UN approved the cease-fire and called upon Iraq to respect boundaries, pay war compensation and destroy chemical, biological and nuclear weapons.

## KATHERINE JENERETTE

Katherine Jenerette took part in 'Desert Storm' as a member of the US Army's 3rd Armoured Division. She was nicknamed 'Desert Kate'. This is part of what she wrote about her experiences:

*Desert Storm was exciting but at the same time in the back of my mind I thought 'I could really die' so it was also very scary.*

*I remember taking our gas masks everywhere – the bathroom, the shower, even when I was out jogging.*

*My adventures included black-out driving through the desert to find a telephone satellite site, feeding cookies to camels, dust storms, **scuds** overhead, keeping as much 5.56 ammo in my web gear as I could carry for my M-16 and, the hardest part, losing a friend killed by a land-mine.*

*What were we really fighting for? US soldiers knew we were fighting to protect America's way of life – OIL. We knew the oil in the Middle East was definitely necessary for our country and our way of life. We were not there to help spread democracy, we were there to ensure that the United States' vital interests in that part of the world were secure.*

## Dag Hammarskjold (1905–61)

Dag Hammarskjold was a Swedish statesman and United Nations official, who worked as the UN Secretary-General for more than eight years.

Before he worked for the United Nations, he was an assistant professor at Stockholm University, chairman of the Bank of Sweden, and Swedish Foreign Secretary.

Hammarskjold was a member of the Swedish delegation to the UN in 1952 and in 1953 was elected Secretary-General. He helped set up the UN Emergency Force in Sinai and Gaza (1956), worked for peace in the Middle East (1957–8), and sent observers into the Lebanon in 1958.

He was involved in negotiations to settle the Congo crisis in 1961 but was killed in an air crash near Ndola in Zambia. He was awarded the Nobel Peace Prize in 1961.

# 3.7 POSTWAR BRITAIN: EARLY CHILDHOOD MEMORIES 1947–52

Memories are an extremely important source of information for historians. Of course, sometimes the memories are inaccurate because a person has not remembered things clearly or did not really know what was going on in the first place.

This unit and the next tell the story of Britain after the war through the eyes of a child living at this time (marked ●) and in the words of an historian (marked ◇).

## Bomb-sites and re-building

● *Everywhere you went in London there were bomb sites. The houses on either side would be shored up and on their outside walls, which were once inside the missing house next door, you could still see wallpaper, fireplaces, and sometimes a shelf or washbasin hanging at a crazy angle. Rosebay willow herb grew all over the ground and in the nooks and crannies of the walls.*

◇ The government backed the production of thousands of pre-fabricated single-storey houses made from steel frames with asbestos panels. The first 'prefab' was put up in 1944. They were meant to last for ten years but some people were still living in them in the 1990s. The government's long-term planning was to build new towns out in the countryside.

## The National Health Service

● *One morning Dad went to see our doctor to ask about the new National Health Service. The doctor said: 'Mr Dawson, I didn't think you wanted that kind of service'. But we joined all the same.*

◇ In 1946 the government passed a National Health Act. This provided free medical, dental and eye care treatment for everyone. It was all paid for from people's taxes. A public opinion survey in 1956 found that 96% of people wanted the new system.

## The Festival of Britain

● *My grandparents took me all over London when I was a child. They wanted to take me to the Festival of Britain. All my friends went. But for some reason Mum and Dad wouldn't let me go and they wouldn't take me themselves. I still don't know why. Gran and Grandpa brought me back a tartan pencil case. It didn't seem the same, somehow!*

◇ The Festival of Britain was held on the south bank of the river Thames in 1951. A fun-fair and exhibition halls, a concert hall, theatre, cafés and restaurants were built and gardens laid out. The Royal Festival Hall and the gardens around it are all that is now left.

## Source A

The Halls and Skylon of the Festival of Britain.

A British Restaurant.

## Shopping and rationing

- *I used to go shopping for my mother. This could sometimes take a whole morning even though the shops were just round the corner. Most of the time was spent queuing – especially for bread and meat. One day word went round that a certain shop had some 'viyella' material. My mother and her friends queued for hours. For years afterwards you would know whose mother was in that queue because the children had dresses and skirts, blouses, shirts and shorts all made from either pale blue or pale pink spotted viyella!*
- ◇ In May 1946 a world wheat shortage led to the rationing of bread, something that hadn't happened even in the darkest days of the war. Gradually, however, wartime rationing ended: clothing, tinned foods and soap in 1949 and 1950; tea in 1952; chocolate, sweets, eggs and sugar in 1953; coke, margarine, butter, cheese, meat and bacon in 1954, and coal in 1958. Other goods were 'rationed' because they were in such short supply.

## Eating out

- *Every week I went with my mother to the British restaurant. It was in a long, low white building by the railway bridge. There was a counter where you queued for your lunch. We sat at wooden trestle tables and the chairs were wooden and folded flat when they weren't being used. I don't know whether or not the restaurant opened every day but we always went on a Thursday.*
- ◇ British restaurants provided cheap, nutritious meals for anyone who needed them. The cost was subsidised by the government.

## Fighting fathers?

- *Friends laughed at me because during the war my Dad joined the Home Guard. At the start it was called the 'Local Defence Volunteers'. My Mum called it the 'Look, Dive and Vanish brigade'. My friend Gillian's father was a dispatch rider in Italy. That was terribly glamorous. When I went round to tea he cooked us marvellous spaghetti bolognese. It was quite different from the spaghetti in tomato sauce I had at home, which came out of tins.*
- ◇ The Local Defence Volunteers (soon called the Home Guard) were formed in 1940 to help in the defence of Britain against German invasion. About 500,000 men were recruited and equipped with British, Canadian and American weapons. The Home Guard also manned anti-aircraft and coastal defences. It was dissolved on 31 December 1944.

## Changing schools

- *When I was in the top class in primary school I took the 11+ examination. We all did. We had been taking practice papers for weeks. This one exam decided which school you went to next. We all wanted to go to grammar school and not just any old grammar school, but the best one in our city. No one wanted to go to a secondary modern school. The results came out two days before my eleventh birthday. I was promised a bike if I passed and a tennis racquet if I didn't. But I found the bike hidden in our shed, so I knew I would get it no matter what happened!*

- In 1944 Parliament passed an Education Act which said that there were to be three types of secondary school: grammar, modern and technical. Children were allocated to the school which would be best for them. In 1965 the Labour government required all local education authorities to submit plans to reorganise their schools as comprehensives. In 1970 the Conservative government said education authorities could choose not to do this, but the move to comprehensives went on.

## Capital punishment

- *In English lessons we often had debates. Someone would be chosen to propose the motion and someone to oppose it. They made formal speeches and then anyone could join in the argument. At the end we voted. Sometimes the debates were on silly topics, like 'This House believes cats make better pets than dogs.' But in 1955 Ruth Ellis was hanged for shooting her lover whom she had discovered was unfaithful to her. We debated the rights and wrongs of capital punishment and the arguments on both sides were passionate and angry. I made up my mind then about what I believed and I haven't changed it since.*

- In 1957 Parliament passed a Homicide Act which abolished hanging except for murderers who killed a police officer, or killed whilst stealing or by shooting or by explosion. In 1965 the death penalty was abolished for five years as an experiment. In 1969 Parliament made the abolition permanent.

## Equal opportunities

- *When we were about sixteen, a woman came to school to tell us about the different careers that were open to girls. They ranged widely, from airline pilot to plumber. But at the end she gave herself away. 'Whatever anyone says', she declared, 'the best jobs for women are nursing and teaching.' Our teachers were furious. They had been working hard to convince us that any career was within our grasp. In one sense they were right. But they never told us of the battles we would have as women in a man's world.*

- In 1970 the Equal Pay Act stated that from 1975 men and women should receive equal treatment in pay and conditions where they were doing similar work, or work which evaluation tests had shown to be comparable. Discrimination through separate pay scales, or separately negotiated agreements affecting only one sex, were illegal. In 1975 Parliament set up the Equal Opportunities Commission, which investigated complaints from people who believed they had been discriminated against because of their sex.

## Source A

The Aldermaston March.

### Protest

- *With some friends I joined the Campaign for Nuclear Disarmament (CND). We wore campaign badges on our blazers until the school banned them. We went to local group meetings and marches. I wanted to go on the big Easter march to Aldermaston, but my parents forbade me. I was furious. In the summer, without telling them, I went to a demonstration in Trafalgar Square. It ended with a sit-down peaceful protest – and we were all taken away in police vans. Luckily I wasn't charged. In those days we believed we could change the world.*

- ◇ The first British hydrogen bomb was tested in May 1957. Other tests followed. In 1963 the USSR, the USA and Great Britain agreed to a test-ban treaty which stopped all testing of nuclear weapons above ground, in outer space or under water. But underground tests were still permitted and nuclear weapons were still part of the **arsenal** of all Great Powers.

### Divorce and pregnancy

- *Two major events happened in my class when I was about fourteen. Mary Machie's mother divorced her father. No one spoke to her about it. It was something so shocking that no one knew what to say. No one's parents got divorced and so something unspeakably dreadful must have happened. In the same year Janet Wilson got pregnant. We listened in fascinated horror to her stories of unsuccessful secret visits to a back-street abortionist and then to rows at home when she had to tell her parents. We watched her gymslip for tell-tale signs of swelling. We wondered when the teachers would find out. One day Janet just wasn't there. We heard that she had been sent to live with an aunt until the baby was born and that her mother was going to bring the baby up as if it was hers. We never saw her again.*

- ◇ In 1967 Parliament passed the Abortion Act, which allowed abortions to be performed legally if there was a threat to the mental or physical health of the mother; if the child was going to be severely handicapped; or if the child was likely to be born into undesirable conditions.

  In 1969 Parliament changed the law about divorce. The only ground for divorce was to be 'irretrievable breakdown' of the marriage. Proof would be separation for two years if both partners agreed; five years if not.

### The Swinging Sixties

The 1960s are often called the 'Swinging Sixties' because young people could do what they liked, wear what they liked and say what they liked – or could they?

87

Modern-day South Africa is a multi-racial society where people of different colours and races are equal in the eyes of the law. But this was not always the case. Indeed until 1994 South Africa was known throughout the world as the country where the Black majority was excluded from having a say in the running of its country by the White minority.

## Early settlement

Until the mid 17th century South Africa was the home of black native Africans. From that time European settlers began to arrive in the Cape. The first settlers were Dutch, but they were soon followed the British who quickly gained control of the area. So the Dutch settlers (usually called Afrikaners) moved north and established two of their own provinces, the Transvaal and the Orange Free State. The British won control of these areas in 1902 and eight years later joined them with the two British provinces, Cape Colony and Natal to form the Union of South Africa.

## White control

Although they made up only 15% of the population of the country, the Whites were in complete control of South Africa. Only Whites could be elected to Parliament and all the best jobs and land were restricted to them. In 1913 the government of the Union passed the Native Land Act which said that black Africans could not own land in 90% of South Africa. They were to be restricted to native reserves and had to carry special passes before they were allowed to enter White areas. Later laws restricted rights for black Africans at work and even forbade them from marrying Whites.

The black Africans formed their own organisation called the African National Congress (ANC) to campaign for equal rights. The ANC believed in non-violent protest, but it soon faced problems which made non-violent protest very difficult.

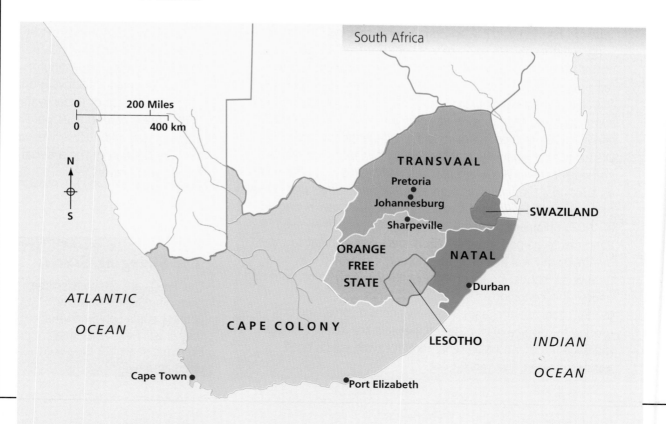

South Africa

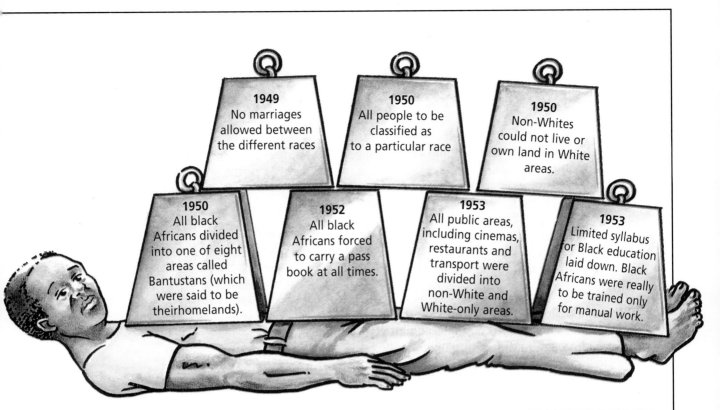

The Establishment of Apartheid 1949-53

**1949** No marriages allowed between the different races

**1950** All people to be classified as to a particular race

**1950** Non-Whites could not live or own land in White areas.

**1950** All black Africans divided into one of eight areas called Bantustans (which were said to be theirhomelands).

**1952** All black Africans forced to carry a pass book at all times.

**1953** All public areas, including cinemas, restaurants and transport were divided into non-White and White-only areas.

**1953** Limited syllabus for Black education laid down. Black Africans were really to be trained only for manual work.

## The establishment of Apartheid

In 1948 the Nationalist Party took office and introduced apartheid in South Africa. That is, it passed laws to ensure that the country was formally separated according to racial type. People in South Africa were classified according to one of four racial groups: Black, White, Asian or Coloured (mixed race). Their rights depended largely upon which group they belonged to. White supremacy was made official and the rights of non-Whites restricted by law.

## Opposition to Apartheid

The non-white population of South Africa was horrified by the introduction of apartheid. In 1950 the ANC called a national strike to protest. Then in 1954 opponents of apartheid drew up the 'Freedom Charter' calling for the ending of apartheid.

In 1960 thousands of opponents of apartheid demonstrated outside a police station at Sharpeville. The police panicked and 67 black Africans were shot dead.

The incident inflamed anti-apartheid opinion and there were widespread demonstrations. The government was forced to impose a state of emergency in which almost 12,000 people were imprisoned without trial. The ANC decided to abandon its policy of non-violence and arrests soon followed, including the ANC President, Chief Albert Luthuli. Two other leading ANC members, Walter Sisulu (imprisoned 1963) and Nelson Mandela (imprisoned 1964) were each to spend 26 years in prison for opposition to apartheid.

During the same period 69 black Africans died as a result of police 'interrogation'. It was said that they had died as a result of accidents such as 'slipping and fatally injuring themselves', but everyone knew what this really meant.

## Source A

An account from a journalist who witnessed events at Sharpeville in 1960.

We heard the chatter of the machine gun, then another. There were people running towards me and I kept on taking pictures as I lay on the grass. Hundreds of women rushed past us. Some of them were laughing; they must have thought that the police were firing blanks. Hundreds of kids were running too. One little boy had an old black coat, which he held up behind his back, thinking perhaps that it might save him from the bullets.

One of the policemen was standing on top of an armoured car firing his machine gun into the crowd. When the firing stopped nobody was moving in our field. They were either wounded or dead. 'Let's go before they get our film', I said.

## Desmond Tutu (1931–)

Desmond Tutu was first ordained as a priest in 1960 and has devoted his life to fighting injustice. In 1978 he became the first black Secretary of the South African Council of Churches and has used his position to attack the system of apartheid.

He supported the use of sanctions against the white South African government and in 1984 was awarded the Nobel Peace Prize in recognition of his opposition to apartheid. After the ending of apartheid he was appointed to chair the Truth and Reconciliation Commission.

## The world reaction

There was widespread opposition to apartheid from around the world, particularly in black countries. In 1960 South Africa was forced to leave the Commonwealth. In 1962 the United Nations imposed a trade boycott on South Africa. But many foreign countries simply found a way round the sanctions. South Africa was wealthy and they wanted to trade with it.

Pressure was also applied through sport. In 1968 the England cricket team was due to tour South Africa. It picked the South-African born mixed race player, Basil D'Oliveira in its team. The South African government said that D'Oliveira would not be welcome and so England cancelled the tour. There were no cricket matches between the two countries for another 25 years. Sport with South Africa became unacceptable to many people and other sports and other countries soon followed the English cricket authorities' lead.

## Apartheid under attack

Despite international opposition apartheid continued and so did the demonstrations

## Source B

Headlines in the English newspaper, the Times in September 1968.

Vorster says MCC team unacceptable in South Africa

...of M.C.C. last night considered ...ll off the tour of South Af... ...frican Prime M9i... ...fountain th...

D'Oliveira 'political cricket ball'

Mr Vorster told a politica... was ready to play h... the team of h... From... of s...

Feeling of disgust over ban

Among cricketers everywhere there will be a fe...

MCC call off tour of South Africa

...'s tour of South Africa is Off. The new ...d's last night between the M. ...of the South Afric...

A cartoon published in a South African newspaper in 1959. On the sign the writing is in English and Afrikaans.

## STEVE BIKO

Steve Biko was a leader of opposition to apartheid who died in police custody in 1977. Biko was one of the founders of a group called the Black Consciousness Movement in the 1960s and was arrested on several occasions before finally being taken into custody in August 1977. He was thirty years old and in good health. One month later he died of brain damage. The police claimed that he hit his head against a wall whilst being restrained. After five days, when it was realised how badly injured he was, he was driven hundreds of kilometres on the floor of a police car to hospital. He did not recover. There was a international outcry, but the official inquest acquitted the police of any wrongdoing. More recently, on 11 September 1997, a police witness admitted to the Truth Commission (see page 92) that Biko died as result of severe beatings from the police.

against it in South Africa. There was particular resentment in the townships (poor areas of towns and cities where black people lived). In 1976 15,000 pupils in a township demonstrated against the government announcement that in future all lessons were to be in Afrikaans. They saw this not only as a foreign language but also as the language of their oppressors. Police opened fire and a number of children were killed. Once more there was an outbreak of violence and once more the government introduced tough measures.

### The beginning of the end

In 1978 P.W. Botha became President. He realised that apartheid could not be maintained by force and decided to win support of those Blacks who had skilled jobs by watering down apartheid. He hoped to be able to divide opposition to apartheid. So he allowed Blacks to buy property in White areas, join unions and receive a better education. He even allowed mixed marriages and abolished the requirement to carry a pass book.

But Botha's reforms did not work. Black Africans wanted equality, not a few changes. In 1983 the United Democratic Front (UDF) was set up to campaign against apartheid and included many Whites. A leading member of the organisation was Archbishop Desmond Tutu. There was also opposition to the government from White extremists such as Eugene Terre Blanche and his Afrikaner Resistance Movement, which opposed any changes to the apartheid system.

## More clashes

Although the UDF opposed violence, rioting became increasingly common and divisions within the Black community were also shown. Chief Buthelezi's Inkatha Party criticised the ANC and there were often clashes between ANC and Inkatha supporters. In places this led to horrific murder by 'necklace'. Some areas of the country became almost ungovernable and Botha was forced to declare a state of emergency once more. Police brutality increased and international opposition to apartheid led to foreign companies withdrawing from South Africa and the tightening up of sanctions. However, Mrs Thatcher argued that sanctions merely harmed Black people and so Britain did not join in the boycott – though thousands of Britons refused to buy South African goods from supermarkets.

## Apartheid ended

In 1989 President Botha resigned through ill health and was replaced by F.W. de Klerk. He realised the need to make concessions to the Blacks. He removed the ban on the ANC and finally released Nelson Mandela from prison in 1990. Mandela then called off ANC's campaign of violence against the government.

The new South African Flag

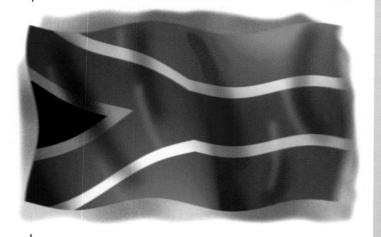

## One man one vote

During 1991 and 1992 talks were held to establish a new constitution based on 'one person one vote'. Not surprisingly these talks proved very difficult and it was only after great efforts by both sides that a 'Record of Understanding' was reached. It was agreed that the first multi-racial elections in South African history would take place in April 1994. Mandela and de Klerk were awarded the Nobel Peace Prize for bringing about the agreement.

## The new government

The results of the 1994 election put the country in the hands of the ANC, which won 62.6% of the vote. Nelson Mandela became President and another ANC representative, Thabo Mbeki, became First Deputy President. F.W. de Klerk's National Party scored the second highest number of votes and he became Second Deputy President. Of the 27 seats in the Cabinet, ANC took 18, the National Party 6 and Inkatha 3.

### The Truth Commission

In 1996 the Truth and Reconciliation Commission began its work in South Africa. Its task was to unearth the truth of the atrocities that had occurred under apartheid and so help the country 'heal its wounds'. In order to get people to testify before it the Commission granted an amnesty to those testifying, so that they would not be frightened to admit what they had done. The commission also heard accounts from the relatives of victims.

But the truth does not always help heal, especially as those testifying are exempt from criminal proceedings. In 1984 the wife and daughter of Marius Schoon were blown apart by a bomb planted by the security forces. Marius now knows that Craig Williamson, a government spy, played a part in the bombing. 'Suddenly their deaths are in the forefront of my mind again,' he says. 'Now it is personal. There is a good chance that I may actually shoot Williamson.'

## The 'Rainbow' country

It was hoped that this new government would lead the new 'rainbow' country to a period of racial harmony and prosperity. The first signs of this came when black and white South Africans stood side by side to cheer their country to victory in the rugby World Cup in 1995. But there is still much work to do and since the formation of the new government both Chief Buthelezi and F.W. de Klerk have resigned because of opposition to ANC policies.

### Nelson Mandela (1918–)

Mandela was for many years the world's most famous political prisoner. In his early years Mandela was groomed to be a chief of the Thembu tribe, but instead he turned his attention to fighting apartheid. He was expelled from college in 1940 for organising a student strike and in 1948 became general secretary of the ANC Youth League. In 1952 he was served with an order banning him from attending meetings but ignored it. He was acquitted on a charge of treason in 1961 but in 1964 was sentenced to life imprisonment. After a world-wide campaign he was released in 1990 and in April 1994 was elected the first black President of the Republic of South Africa.

### Source E

An article from the English newspaper, *The Guardian*, 27 February 1998.

#### SECURITY POLICE PLOTTED MANDELA ASSASSINATION

It has been alleged that members of South Africa's now disbanded security forces hired an extremist hitman to shoot Nelson Mandela at his presidential inauguration ceremony in front of world-wide television audiences in 1994.

The extraordinary story emerged after an informer admitted to Archbishop Desmond Tutu's Truth Commission that he was hired for £31,000 to shoot Mr Mandela in an assassination which would have stunned the world and probably resulted in civil war. He pulled out after he heard that security officers planned to shoot him immediately after the assassination and then claim the credit.

Detectives investigating the claims are said to have arrested a senior police officer and seized two high-powered rifles.

# GLOSSARY

**abdicate** stand down from power.

**appeasement** calm down an enemy by making concessions to them.

**armistice** a stopping of war, by a truce made by both opposing sides.

**arsenal** the store of weapons held by a person or government.

**billeted** placed with families whom the government had asked to look after the evacuees.

**black market** selling hard-to-get goods (especially those on ration) illegally.

**blitzkrieg** a sudden and heavy military attack, done to gain a quick victory.

**buffer zone** an area of safety.

**bund** a Jewish socialist organisation set up in 1897 in Vilna, Poland. It supported and organised workers, upheld cultural rights, formed self-defence squads and worked actively against anti-Semitism.

**collaborate** work together with.

**Communist** someone who believes in Communism. Communism was a theory of government developed by Karl Marx. He believed that war between the classes should lead to a state where everything is publicly owned and shared out according to what people need.

**consolidate** make strong and stable.

**convoys** groups of vehicles travelling together.

**democratic** in favour of social equality.

**dictator** someone who rules alone with total authority.

**fascist** someone who was in favour of fascism. Fascism was a very right-wing **nationalist** movement.

**guerrilla** an unofficial soldier, usually a member of a political group, who takes part in sabotage and ambushes instead of conventional war.

**hyper-inflation** excessively high inflation in prices.

**militant** aggressively active, especially in relation to politics.

**military sanctions** military action imposed on one country by another, to try and make the first country conform to a set of rules or a way of government.

**nationalist** an extreme patriot

**police state** a state controlled by political police who oversee all activities.

**propaganda** publicity specially selected to put forward one point of view, usually political.

**purser** the officer in charge of the accounts on a ship.

**radar** a system whereby objects can be detected even when they are far away, by bouncing radio waves off them.

**recession** when the economy is doing badly.

**reparations** an amount paid out to make amends for something. Countries pay reparations after war as a punishment.

**republic** a state in which power is held by the people, or their elected leaders, instead of a monarch or supreme leader.

**scapegoats** people to blame for something, even though it wasn't their fault.

**scuds** short range missiles of mass destruction.

**subversion** seeking to overthrow a government or regime.

**totalitarian** a **dictator** style of government.

**tribunal** a board set up to judge over a matter of public concern.

# INDEX